DATE DUE

DEMCO 38-297

The Slow Learner

The Slow Learner

WILLARD ABRAHAM

*Chairman, Department of Educational Services
and Coordinator, Special Education
Arizona State University*

The Center for Applied Research in Education, Inc.
New York

Foreword

Not everyone who is earnestly concerned about the slow learner clearly understands him, unequivocally identifies him, or advocates sound programs for dealing with him. The term "slow learner" implies generalized retardation in all types of learning. But when we ponder more carefully, we find that the term might be rephrased as "subaverage (for age) reader." Since reading is the key to so much learning, and since promotions naïvely assume equal pacing, this oversimplification is too readily accepted; and since school progress is principally based on verbal intellectual requirements, the scholastic bias is understandable, although it is unacceptable.

With characteristic insight and judgment Dr. Willard Abraham moves from these narrow views to broader concepts of definition, identification, causative variables, and imaginative programs. He notes that I.Q. is only one variable, and a rather dubious one; that M.A. is more meaningful than I.Q. and that both are related to types of tests and test circumstances; that many factors other than verbal intelligence influence slow learning; that slow is not necessarily poor; that these components may be dealt with remediably; that I.Q. or M.A. and learning are not directly equatable; that learning is measured directly as achievement and only hypothetically as verbal "intelligence."

In short, the slow learner is behind schedule in learning *something* rather than everything. Even generalized slow learners may learn rapidly in some areas, just as generalized rapid learners may learn slowly in some tasks. Indeed, one of Dr. Abraham's specially significant passages is on the academic slow learner with high I.Q. Hence, we do well to precede "slow learner" with an adjective denoting the learning task; and certainly we should not identify this with M.A. or I.Q. alone.

Dr. Abraham does not harass his reader with these arguments. Rather, he leads the reader gently and without bickering or persuasion to a sympathetic understanding of school learning and its difficulties. Being school oriented, he offers explicit material on all phases of slow learning and slow learners at school and with relation to home, community, and personal programs.

This is a refreshing and informing exposition of a major school problem. It is accomplished with the sympathy, clarity, understanding, and practicality that marks this author's many contributions to the education of exceptional children. The reader will enjoy the direct style and the concise, yet thorough, coverage.

EDGAR A. DOLL

Consulting Psychologist
Bellingham, Washington Public Schools

The Slow Learner

Willard Abraham

Dr. Abraham's book on *The Slow Learner* is in many respects a complementary volume in the Library of Education to Dr. De Haan's *Accelerated Learning Programs*. Increased knowledge by psychologists of individual differences has been the driving force behind the identification of the slow learner, the recognition of his special problems, and the development of programs suited to his needs and abilities. The serious implications for the family, classroom, and community of the failure of our educational system to "do something" about slow learners who have poor ability and also those who are bright but operate below their level of ability are stressed by the author.

Special efforts are made by Dr. Abraham to describe the characteristics and ways of early identification of the slow learner. Included are discussions about the parent's problems, community resources, work opportunities, relationship to juvenile delinquency, and the role of the federal government. Dr. Abraham describes the efforts of the public schools to handle this problem and includes considerable detail about the organization, current practices, curriculum, and teaching techniques.

In very informative appendices he presents an illustrative case study of a slow learner and two sample programs from communities which make special attempts to come to grips with the problems of the slow learner. In looking at the future, Dr. Abraham is optimistic about the ability of our school system to identify and provide for the needs of this large proportion of our school population, the slow learner.

ERIC F. GARDNER
Content Editor

Contents

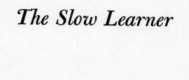

The Slow Learner

CHAPTER I

The Problem

The American philosophy of education, based on educating every child to his capacity, cannot afford to make exceptions. The loss of potential manpower, the high drop-out rate from our schools, the cost of unemployment, delinquency, and crime, the threat to sound family relationships and to individuals within families—all are direct or indirect consequences which can be traced, at least partly, to the fact that education has largely ignored the needs of an important segment of our society: the children often referred to as "slow learners."

> The education of the mentally well-endowed has been a vexing problem, but that of the deviate of subnormal learning capability has been stated to be among the most pressing faced by the public school today.[1]

Educational, Sociological, and Psychological Aspects

Because slow learners will become a significant part of our future citizenry (with important jobs of an occupational, family, and social nature to perform), this ignoring of needs must be noted, studied, and discussed. Efforts must also be made to offer practical solutions. These children do not constitute a minor problem—not when one observes the thousands of classrooms they attend, the conferences of teachers and administrators almost perpetually faced with the problem, the parents for whom it is a source of concern, and the communities bearing the cost of educating them and paying a larger price later if the education provided is inadequate.

If anyone doubts the need of sincere efforts to educate these slow learners, let him meditate on the fact that twenty out of every hun-

---

[1] Georgia Lightfoot, *Personality Characteristics of Bright and Dull Children* (New York: Bureau of Publications, Teachers College, Columbia University, 1951), p. 107.

1

2 THE PROBLEM

dred pupils chosen at random means at least four million for the country as a whole. Then let him ponder the consequences for the general welfare of permitting that number of future adult citizens to grow up illiterate, uncultured, and uninitiated in the American way of life. If anyone doubts the soundness of investing a considerable sum in their education, let him try to forecast the consequences of *not* making that investment, bearing in mind, of course, diminished capacity to produce as well as to consume, but more important, not overlooking the declining zeal for the democratic way of life that invariably accompanies illiteracy and ignorance.[2]

In the editor's introduction to *Teaching the Slow Learner,* a strong point is succinctly made by Hollis L. Caswell:

> . . . the education these slow-learning children acquire is of major importance to American democracy. . . . They will do their share of the work of the world, they will cast their votes, they will participate in the activities of labor unions and farm organizations, they will make homes. What they become, the ideas they develop, are vital to our national welfare.[3]

Administrators and others in the field of special education have not accepted sufficient responsibility for the slow learners because ". . . they do not deviate sufficiently from the normal to be considered exceptional and thus come within the province of the education of mentally handicapped children."[4] With our increasing school population, more children will be in the slow learning category, and more will need the parental help and understanding, the school programs, the teachers, and the community concern discussed in the pages that follow. More, however, will be able to profit from the newer approaches and future possibilities related to living and working with these children.

A far smaller number, the mentally retarded, have received greater attention through research, writing, and organizations than have the slow learners. Current attention to education must be large enough to encompass the slow learners also, to draw attention to their needs, to suggest program adaptations, and to help develop them to capacities which are often unrecognized.

[2] W. B. Featherstone, *Teaching the Slow Learner* (New York: Bureau of Publications, Teachers College, Columbia University, 1941), pp. vii-viii.

[3] *Ibid.,* p. v.

[4] G. Orville Johnson, *The Slow Learner—A Second-Class Citizen?* The J. Richard Street Lecture for 1962 (Syracuse, N.Y.: Syracuse University, 1962), p. 10.

Definitions

Some writers in the field of special education use I.Q. exclusively in describing slow learners (and may not be consistent in their numerical limitations). Others confuse the issue because of awkward terminology, and still others contribute unclear thinking induced by vague discussions of aptitudes, talents, achievement, abilities, and intelligence. I.Q.'s of 80 to 95, 85 or less, 70 to 89, 50 to 75, and 50 to 89 are found in the literature on this subject. Terms like the following appear: borderline, borderline retarded, low normal, dull, dull normal, mildly handicapped, dullards, backward, nonacademic.

One source referred to "island children," the ones who "are surrounded and isolated in our educational hierarchy." [5] Agreement is fairly general that these children constitute 15 to 20 per cent of our school population, although the term "slow learner" is sometimes used to apply to all levels of mental retardation, or just to the educable levels (the 50–75 I.Q. group). Among the specific and somewhat representative definitions which appear in the literature on this subject are the following:

> . . . distinctly below average in intellectual capacity . . . between 70 and 89 (intelligence quotient) . . . usually among the lowest 15 to 20 per cent of the students in general intelligence.[6]

> These children are unable to satisfy regular grade standards year by year and are retarded in their academic achievement for their age group.[7]

> . . . we may define a child who is educationally subnormal as one whose educational attainments are less than 80 per cent of what is normal for his years.[8]

> The slow-learning child is a child whose mental ability is high enough to justify keeping him in the regular classroom but low enough to give him considerable difficulty in keeping up with the average speed of the class.[9]

---

[5] Irving Bloom and Walter I. Murray, "Some Basic Issues in Teaching Slow Learners," *Understanding the Child,* XXVI, No. 3 (June, 1957), p. 85.

[6] Thomas J. Frain, *Administrative and Instructional Provisions for Rapid and Slow Learners in Catholic Secondary Schools* (Washington, D.C.: The Catholic University of America Press, 1956), p. 13.

[7] Christine Ingram, *Education of the Slow-Learning Child* (New York: The Ronald Press Company, 1960), p. 13.

[8] Cyril Burt, *The Causes and Treatment of Backwardness* (New York: Philosophical Library, 1953), p. 38.

[9] Robert F. DeHaan and Jack Kough, *Helping Children With Special Needs,* elementary school ed., Vol. II (Chicago: Science Research Associates, 1956), p. 152.

4 THE PROBLEM

The slow learners . . . usually find the traditional type of school program too difficult to handle without some modifications of the program to adjust requirements to their normal capacity for achievement. . . . The appropriate designation to be given to the group which stands between the mentally deficient and the normal is still a question. They are frequently referred to as the "slow learners." [10]

. . . children whose measured intelligence quotient is somewhere between 80 and 95. . . . The general tendency at the present time, however, is to face reality with parents and educators, and thus the term slow learner is rapidly becoming restricted to the higher group referred to previously . . .[11]

Ordinarily, "slow-learningness" or "slow learner" refers to the capacity of an individual to learn intellectual things—the kind of capacity that is measured by verbal tests. At best the term is a rather euphemistic and unsatisfactory one.[12]

For a basic point of departure, the following ingredients of a descriptive definition are proposed:

1. The intelligence range is approximately 75 to 90 I.Q., but keep in mind the limitations of tests and testing personnel and the variations in scores, depending on what test is used, who administers it, when it is given, and other factors—or performance at the 75 to 90 I.Q. level despite indications of higher capabilities. These I.Q. levels should not be rigidly limited, however.

2. The inaccurate reflection of intelligence may be due to one or more limitations or variations, related to factors such as family and home, neighborhood, culture, language, socio-economic condition, or school.

3. These may be the children in a regular classroom who do not quite keep up in the early grades (and lag behind even more later on), but who are not consistent in their development; human growth is along a continuum, rather than in neat groups.

4. These children are usually slow in intellectual matters, but not necessarily slow to the same extent in artistic, mechanical, or social activities.

---

[10] National Society for the Study of Education, *The Education of Exceptional Children*, 49th Yearbook, Part II (Chicago: The Society, 1950), Chap. XIII, p. 238.
[11] William M. Cruickshank and G. Orville Johnson, eds., *Education of Exceptional Children and Youth* (Englewood Cliffs, N.J.: Prentice-Hall, Inc., 1958), p. 4.
[12] Featherstone, *op. cit.*, p. 2.

5. A substantial segment of this monograph is devoted to a large group of children seldom classified in the professional literature as "slow learners," but they literally are. Although potentially gifted, they function as slow learners. Because their neglect is tragic not only for them but also for the society that needs their abilities, the problem is singled out for special consideration in some detail.

A distinction may be made between generalized slowness and retardation in specific fields. "There are many different areas and ways of learning and anyone may be a slow learner in some areas, yet rapid in others. The old rhyme says: 'One could whistle, and one could sing, and the other could play the violin.' This refers to the successful learning differences, but implies that people are not equally successful in all directions." [13]

Although everyone may be described as a slow learner in one or more ways—for example, failing to learn in proportion to his desires, efforts, or instruction—[14] the major emphasis in this section will be on the children who achieve below their inferred ability because of individual rates of maturation, environmental variables, limitations in testing, or possible multiple factors.

Common Misunderstandings

Even in recent years a number of misconceptions and misunderstandings have persisted among parents, teachers, and others in their discussions of slow learners. These misconceptions should be corrected before going into causes, characteristics, and identification techniques related to these children.

For example, many people still believe that an I.Q. is immobile, unchangeable, and set for all time. They do not recognize the influences of a rich or barren environment as contributing toward raising an intelligence capacity or lowering to a new intelligence floor. Another idea which may be comforting, but untrue, is that a child who is slow in one area is necessarily higher in others, perhaps even higher than the average person. Such compensation does not necessarily develop among human characteristics, for weakness in one

---

[13] Edgar A. Doll, "Varieties of Slow-Learners," *Exceptional Children*, No. 2 (November, 1953), p. 61.

[14] *Ibid.*, p. 86.

area is not weighted by strength in another. Nor is there a balance established between verbal abilities (low) and nonverbal ones (high), or book-mindedness (low) and hand-mindedness (high). Hand activities may provide an area of reasonable success because of their concrete, meaningful nature rather than as a compensating factor for low academic abilities; they also may develop, of course, because of the longer time put into them.

Slow learners do not balance their lower intellectual abilities with greater height and strength. This misconception sometimes stems from the fact that they are the tallest and huskiest in their classrooms, an easy matter to understand when one also notes that they may be the oldest because of nonpromotion.

A rather common misunderstanding is associated with slow learners as potential delinquents. It could more accurately be stated that all children are potential delinquents, with the possibility of becoming one directly related to a combination of factors such as environmental conditions (home and community) and frequency of being caught during or after the act. Because the environment of many slow learners is conducive to delinquent behavior, it may more accurately be assumed that in some cases the cause of one is at least partly responsible for the other.

It is important to distinguish between those whose backwardness is innate and permanent and those with accidental, acquired, and correctable traits. One would be mistaken in assuming that the former are slow but will catch up in time. Equally erroneous in the latter situation would be the assumption that all slowness is unalterable. Emphasis must be directed toward the individual and his own potentialities, rather than permit conclusions to be drawn on the basis of generalizations from studies of large groups. One writer said that "the average normal person has more of a blurred picture of the slow child than the slow child has of the world, and of his place in it." [15]

Causes

The causes of mental and academic slowness in children may be traced to two major areas which are usually intertwined: the mental capacity that is inherited and the influence of environmental factors.

[15] Marion Funk Smith, *Teaching the Slow Learning Child* (New York: Harper & Row, Publishers, 1954), p. 16.

Research in medicine and biochemistry may, in time, bring more understanding of the inherited qualities of human beings.[16] As we make progress in discerning causes related to prenatal development, as well as to parents as "carriers" of factors involved in intellectual limitations, solutions of either limited or extensive dimensions will evolve. They will be based on prevention, medication, diet, and surgery. Advances already made in some of the categories of mental retardation are promising as far as other less severe mental limitations are concerned. There are children who are developing normally today, when a few years ago they would have been classified as victims of phenylketonuria, hypothyroidism, galactosemia, hypoglycemia, or kernicterus.[17] Research is also making promising strides as it relates to the causes and prevention of mongolism.[18] "A preventive now being awaited with eagerness is the forthcoming measles vaccine. A considerable group of children are stricken with mental retardation each year when their measles turn into encephalitis." [19]

Some of the claims and hopes are tempered with caution. "The current controversy over the implications of minimal cerebral dysfunction does not promise to be resolved in the foreseeable future. The full significance of this type of impairment is not yet known and must await the time when the medical, para-medical, and educational disciplines have learned to communicate with and complement each other." [20]

Eames describes studies supporting the idea that between the fields of neurology and endocrinology there is a definite relationship which has considerable bearing on the ability to learn.[21] Penfield's research [22] related to memory is another example of the work con-

[16] For example, the research of Dr. Linus Pauling, California Institute of Technology, *Time* (February 2, 1962), p. 37.

[17] Willard Abraham, "These Kinds of Mental Retardation are Preventable," *Midwest Magazine* (September 17, 1961).

[18] Elizabeth Boggs, "Mongolism, New Discoveries Every Month," *Children Limited* (April, 1962), pp. 6–9.

[19] Robert W. Collett, M.D., "We're Winning the War on Mental Retardation," *This Week Magazine* (October 21, 1962).

[20] Raymond L. Clemmens, M.D., "Minimal Brain Damage in Children," *Children*, Vol. 8, No. 5 (September-October, 1961), pp. 179–84.

[21] Thomas H. Eames, "Some Neural and Glandular Bases of Learning," *Journal of Education*, Boston University, Vol. 142, No. 4 (April, 1960), p. 33.

[22] W. Penfield, "The Interpretive Cortex," *Science*, Vol. 129 (June 26, 1959), pp. 1719–25.

nected with learning disabilities for individual children whose performance is often categorized as that of a slow child. Masland, Sarason, and Gladwin point out the limitations of present psychological tests as aids in the diagnosis of brain injury. These tests will have to be much more developed before they can provide a valid criterion in the absence of positive neurological signs.[23]

A large number of individual and combined causes are readily recognized by sociologists, educators, and parents. The clear relationship between them and a child's slowness implies that removal or modification of the difficulty may help elevate the achievement level of the child and perhaps even bring it up to the normal range. The extent or degree of the problem and the length of time it has existed are items inevitably involved in possible correction.

Attributing slowness to intellectual limitations should not necessarily be a first step in stating a cause. Even more likely as a causation factor may be one or more of the conditions itemized below:

1. Socio-economic limitations. Conant[24] and Sexton[25] have presented findings to show the influence of such factors on children's performance in school. Johnson has pointed to these limitations as resulting in "second-class citizens."[26]

2. Cultural and language deprivations or differences. Frank Riessman in *The Culturally Deprived Child* makes a strong plea for the need to understand the culture of the underprivileged, including the positive aspects, such as child-rearing practices, humor, human relationships, and enjoyment of music.

3. Physical factors based on sight, hearing, immature development, malnutrition, or other health conditions. "Behavior and personality are related both to rate of development, or developmental status, and to physique and size."[27] Present research related to the problems of adequately screening children with abnormal ear conditions may be helpful in locating those children who have unwittingly been handicapped because of the fact that present audiometric

[23] Richard L. Masland, Seymour B. Sarason, and Thomas Gladwin, *Mental Subnormality* (New York: Basic Books, Inc., 1960), pp. 363–73.
[24] James B. Conant, *Slums and Suburbs* (New York: McGraw-Hill, Inc., 1961).
[25] Patricia Cayo Sexton, *Education and Income* (New York: The Viking Press, Inc., 1961).
[26] Johnson, *op. cit.*, pp. 16–17.
[27] William E. Martin and Celia Burns Stendler, *Child Behavior and Development* (New York: Harcourt, Brace & World, Inc., 1959), p. 472.

screening in common use cannot identify many children with probably chronic serious otitis media.[28]

4. Family problems or tensions, anxieties, quarrels, excessive
mobility, lack of acceptance of child. Factors in parent-child relationships often raise questions that have no simple answers. Individual patterns of the child's "coping behavior" were the object of
a study by Lois B. Murphy, whose findings add new dimensions to
our knowledge of parent-child relationships.[29] The factor of parent-
child compatibility is an area which sometimes becomes the focal
point when social service agencies in the community are involved
in helping the "neglected child." Families often need services which
would have helped to prevent or overcome problems leading to
child neglect by providing parents with help before the situation
becomes so bad that court action may be involved.[30]

5. School-related factors such as irregular attendance, inefficient
teaching, distaste for school, poor study habits, repeated failure,
and inadequate curriculum. Details of such factors are in the literature related to the migrant child,[31] the drop-out,[32] and the research
on learning[33] and its implications for curriculum and administration.

6. Meager or barren educational resources in home and/or community. Conant points out that while the same methods are used in
all the city elementary schools in a city, the average grade level of
reading in the sixth grade, for example, may vary as much as two
grades from one school to another. He points out the relation of the

[28] Eldon L. Eagles, M.D., Director, Longitudinal Study sponsored by Subcommittee on Hearing in Children of the American Academy of Ophthalmology and
Otolaryngology and by the Children's Bureau, University of Pittsburgh Schools
of Public Health and Medicine, *Children*, Vol. 8, No. 5 (September-October,
1961), p. 195.

[29] Lois Barclay Murphy, *The Widening World of Childhood* (New York: Basic
Books, Inc., 1962).

[30] Annie Lee Sandusky, "Services to Neglected Children," *Children*, Vol. 7,
No. 1 (January-February, 1960), pp. 23–28.

[31] United States Senate, Committee on Labor and Public Welfare, Subcommittee on Education, *Educational Assistance to Migrant Agricultural Employees
and Their Children* (Washington, D.C.: Government Printing Office, 1960).

[32] Harold J. Dillon, *Early School Leavers—A Major Educational Problem* (New
York: National Child Labor Committee, 1949).

[33] Arden N. Frandsen, *How Children Learn* (New York: McGraw-Hill, Inc.,
1957).

reading problem to the socio-economic and cultural level of the home.[34]

7. Incongruities among factors of ability, achievement, and aspiration as they relate to each other. The wide scatter which the psychologist sometimes notes on test scores often goes without further diagnosis or educational planning. A child thus may become by default a member of a class for mentally retarded children when all else appears to have failed to meet his needs in regular classes.

8. Accidents, infections, or diseases resulting in physical or emotional problems. Social welfare workers well know the familiar pattern of the less intelligent clients who form a high percentage of the statistics related to the above factors. Ensuing trauma and debilitating factors pursue many of these families year after year.

9. Inappropriate educational pressures before the child is ready. When the "teachable moment" has been bypassed and the child's normal motivation for learning at his developmental level has been ignored, serious consequences result.

10. Emotional disturbances related to above or other factors. Eli M. Bower,[35] in his speech at the White House Conference on Children and Youth in 1960, stated the importance of early identification as important: "There is little doubt that emotional maladjustment or adjustment cannot be studied as a discrete illness such as pneumonia or scarlet fever. It can only be regarded as a complex, interwoven relationship of the organism with himself and his environment. . . . research points to the fact that teachers, pediatricians, and others can, with some help, make good judgments about the adjustment capacities of children. The problem is how to synthesize the different kinds of information and put the various perceptual parts, like Humpty-Dumpty, back together again." [36]

11. The absence of drive, inner urge, or motivation, existent but not traceable to any of the factors listed above. Teachers, agencies, physicians and neighbors can often suggest what might well be the real reason for a child's problem when the symptoms fit into what an article in the *Saturday Evening Post* called the "battered child

---

[34] Conant, *op. cit.*, p. 24.

[35] White House Conference on Children and Youth, *Reference Papers on Children and Youth* (Washington, D.C.: Government Printing Office, 1960), pp. 231, 239.

[36] *Ibid.*, p. 239.

syndrome," [37] and what is otherwise labeled "neglect and abuse." [38]

The causation problem becomes more complicated when one recognizes that many thousands of children who possess one or a combination of these factors are not slow learners. A "plus factor" thus enters the picture. There is a need for recognizing that slowness does not inevitably result from a particular setting or circumstance, but is the outcome of an inherited quality and/or environmental conditions as they join and affect a child.

Adding to the difficulties are increasingly involved problems of parental despair and subjectivity, teacher pressures more intensively applied to a child because of limited time and increased responsibilities (and despite dedication), and the instilled feeling that one cannot learn. Recognizing the causes and adapting solutions to them are basic in our approach to the slow child.

Pseudo Slow Learning

A distinction must be made between slow learning due to inherent causes and the kind due to our own limitations of evaluation or environment. When a child performs in the 75 to 90 I.Q. range because he is cerebral palsied and has limited manipulative skills, a correction factor must be considered before judgments are made. When a child with a language problem or from a culture different from that on which a particular test was validated acquires a low score, additional work must be done to secure an accurate evaluation for him. Merely translating the test into his language may not be sufficient, because of his cultural and socio-economic deviations. Of course, it is important to remember that in some cases our inadequacies may be the major factor involved, but in other cases the children may actually be slow-learning due to various identifiable reasons.

Additional areas of pseudo slow learning include bright children, working not only beneath their capacity but also below the so-called normal, and children with emotional or physical problems. Individualized educational programs based on accurate child study are

---

[37] Charles Flato, "Parents Who Beat Children," *Saturday Evening Post* (October 6, 1962), pp. 30–35.
[38] Sandusky, *loc. cit.*

needed for these children as well as for all others performing at a
slower than average rate.

The following excerpt is from the abstract based on a recent
major research project which reported on the "pseudo" factors
among a group of so-called bilingual children. Because of the significance and recency of this study and its implications for parts of
this discussion, the objectives, procedures, and findings are quoted
at some length:

That each child is entitled to an education to the limits of his intellectual capacity, as great or as limited as that capacity may be, is a
belief most people hold as part of the American way of life. Implied in
that belief is that there is a means to identify, measure, and evaluate the
intellectual capacity possessed by each child. However, the fields of
psychology and education have long recognized limitations faced in in-
vestigating accurately the capabilities and potentialities for learning which
some children possess.

One group that has frequently been penalized through erroneous
testing and test interpretation is the so-called bilingual category, the children who in the early years are frequently "unilingual" but in a language
other than English. The second language is often accompanied by a
second culture and also an awareness of a different socio-economic
group, one represented by teachers and administrators.

Their language, cultural and socio-economic differences may be re-
flected in school records that seem to indicate mental limitations. Are
such limitations real or pseudo? It is with that problem that this study has
basically occupied itself.

Perhaps through this effort at describing and explaining these children
and their homes, schools, and communities in a longitudinal manner,
some new insights and understandings will evolve, some adjustments will
be made in school programs in which these children are involved, and
some adaptations will be made in the teacher preparation programs
which produce the teachers with whom these children study.

This project consisted primarily of collecting, examining, organizing,
and evaluating pertinent data from a sample of 188 bilingual children,
and identifying factors related to mental retardation and/or pseudo
mental retardation. Through interviews, observations, and tests carefully
selected for this study, in addition to instruments especially developed
for it, such evidence was gathered. It was accumulated from home,
school and community, and from the children themselves, their parents,
teachers, school administrators, community personnel, and consultants
knowledgeable in the field of bilingualism. . . .

The need for this study, and for others which its professional participants hopefully anticipate that it might encourage, is apparent in facts available in the literature of this field. Any one of the following is an adequate reason for continuing study of the problems involved:

1. A high educational drop-out rate for bilingual children as a whole.

2. Low parental vocational aspirations for many of these children.

3. Limited and erroneous information of teachers and administrators about the learning capacities and family backgrounds of these children.

4. Need for continually evaluating and adapting methods of teaching and child study.

5. Implications available in the study of a selected group of bilingual children that extend to all groups of bilingual children wherever they are located and to *all* groups of children whose socio-economic, cultural, and language differences affect their learning and educational programs. . . .

On the basis of test data and other information accumulated about the children in the study, the following findings emerged which provide insights into their lives at home and at school, their total environments, and perhaps their future as well:

1. The median number of siblings per family in the study was approximately twice the national average, and more than nine per cent of the children came from families with 10 or more children.

2. Almost 10 per cent of the fathers for whom information was available had no schooling, and only four per cent had completed high school.

3. The median family income of $2161 placed these families in the lowest quartile nationally, with 50 per cent of the children from homes with annual family incomes of $1686 to $3900. The income range was $900 to $8000, and the source of support extended from public assistance, part-time cotton picking and other unskilled jobs to full-time employment in the skilled crafts and business ownership.

4. In one school the children on the average were retarded a full year on the basis of age in grade when they entered first grade. In all three schools studied the children were behind their contemporaries academically by the time they reached second grade.

5. Bilingual children included in this study appeared to be retarded in both achievement (reading, language, and arithmetic) and ability (performance and verbal).

6. Achievement test scores varied from one subject area to another. The median grade points on reading tests were lower than expected grade levels to the following extent: .15 in second grade;

.60 in third grade; 1.5 in fourth grade. In the California Achievement Test administered in fourth grade, a greater deficiency was found in reading vocabulary than in reading comprehension. Arithmetic achievement varied from .1 to 1.17 grade placement below expectation and English usage, grammar and spelling from .2 above to 1.00 grade placement below expectation, neither with any clear pattern of change. . . .

7. The children scored higher on performance scales than on verbal scale of intelligence tests. However, even the performance test scores were below average, deviating about as much as is found for other economically low groups. . . .

8. The usual positive relationship between performance on tests of mental abiilty and school accomplishment was not found. Test results for these children probably should not be interpreted apart from other information and data from individual case studies. Teachers and others who work with these children should probably not rationalize that a lack of accomplishment results from lack of native ability as measured by the usual tests.

9. The following relationships were found in studying these children in their total setting:

    a. Higher I.Q. scores in both performance and verbal tests were found for children who, as a group, represented the top socio-economic families among those studied.

    b. Higher achievement in both English and arithmetic was found for children who, as a group, represented the top socio-economic families among those studied.

    c. Children from the higher socio-economic families did not demonstrate a higher achievement in reading than did children from other backgrounds.

    d. No important differences were discerned in intelligence or achievement of the children when the children's families were divided on the basis of cohesiveness.

    e. Higher I.Q. scores in both performance and verbal tests were found for children from smaller families, but the differences were slight.

    f. Higher I.Q. scores in both performance and verbal tests were found for children whose fathers had received more education and whose families participated most actively in community affairs.

    g. The definitely bilingual and the definitely unilingual children demonstrated higher performance in both I.Q. and achievement tests than did children with average or below average facility with two languages. . . .

Early in this study a series of five tenets of education in this country were stated. Now that the situation of the bilingual children involved in this project has been described, the importance of these tenets can be seen in bold relief as they apply to these children. No exceptions can be made, no group ignored, no child overlooked—and no country in its period of greatest prosperity and stature can afford to do less than recognize these beliefs as they apply specifically to each child, no matter where he lives, what his father does, what his family thinks about the educational process, or what his future holds for him vocationally.

If taken seriously, if viewed objectively, if spoken meaningfully, these tenets stand as a theme of the future for these and all children:

1. Education for *all* youth.
2. Education is *everybody's* responsibility.
3. Education has the task of helping each child reach his greatest potentiality.
4. Schools are the agencies of the citizenry whom they serve.
5. Education has the task of transmitting the quality features of the culture which surrounds it to present and future generations.

Such beliefs imply the removal of impediments, the awareness of individual problems, the belief in educational oportunity on the basis of need and ability, and the objective, careful, professional recognition of that need and ability as they pertain to each child.

To do any less is to deprive a nation of much of its underdeveloped human resources. To ignore much of the evidence now available is to use evaluative instruments and perpetuate attitudes that mitigate against educating some children to their real capacities. Whether or not the actual label of mental retardation is used, the practice of accepting the idea without questioning its validity may result in a loss to all of us of those maximal contributions that can be made only if individuals are recognized in the framework of their capabilities and potentialities.

In an era when the ways and means are available for a fair and full appraisal and evaluation of each child, it is incumbent on those in the education profession, and all who are in the broader communities that support our schools, to recognize realistically the value to all of viewing every child for what he is and can become. Such recognition demands that a constant questioning spirit be applied to the total environment of bilingual children, to the preparation of their teachers, and to new methods of child study, teaching and understanding the child in his manifold circumstances as such methods evolve in the future.

The current study can answer a few questions but ask many more, solve a few problems but open the door to countless others, satisfy a few differences of opinion but create many additional ones. Piece by piece the questions, problems, and opinions will fall into place. The effort here is to help speed such activities for these children whose educational opportunities occur only once and who are frequently victims of neglect, misunderstanding, and misinformation.[39]

In concluding the discussion of the "pseudo factor" as it relates to slow learners, the point must be made that slow learning may actually be far removed from the inherent abilities of the child and based, instead, on matters of the type investigated in the preceding report of descriptive research.

---

[39] Arizona State University, *Investigation of Mental Retardation and Pseudo-Mental Retardation in Relation to Bilingual and Sub-Cultural. Factors* (Tempe, Arizona: University Bookstore, Arizona State University, 1960). Research performed pursuant to a contract with the United States Department of Health, Education, and Welfare.

CHAPTER II

The Slow Learner

Just as with any large group of average or above average children or adults, slow learners are varied in their physical and emotional characteristics and development. No single trait describes them other than the one of learning more slowly and to a lesser degree. Nor can one tell by appearance or by superficial observation of performance; teachers of Edison, Newton, and others tried and failed. Slowness in school as a single factor is not sufficient either, for in another educational setting the child may perform on an average level.

Although our concern here is not essentially with the person referred to as a "late bloomer," schools have become increasingly aware in recent years of such individuals. They are the ones who show only limited signs of higher intelligence in their early development, but they show an intellectual spurt as the years pass.

Characteristics

The differences of actual slow learners from other children may be in degree rather than in kind, with variations existing among all of us. As Plato said, ". . . it occurs to me myself that to begin with our several natures are not all alike but different. One man is naturally fitted for one task, and another for another." [1]

It is more difficult to recognize the slow learner than to recognize the gifted child. While the gifted child attracts us because he accomplishes rather special things, the slow learner may also be identified through observations of all the things he doesn't do that we expect of him. At first glance he appears just like the other children in his group, and he often gets tagged "lazy" or "poorly motivated." [2]

---

[1] Plato, *The Republic*, Book I.
[2] J. Murray Lee and Dorris May Lee, *The Child and His Development* (New York: Appleton-Century-Crofts, Inc., 1958), p. 326.

Although some writers state that slow learners are essentially normal in their emotional, social, physical, and motor development, others point out many differences. Following are some that are most frequently cited, in comparison with children considered intellectually normal:

1. Short attention and interest span.
2. Limited imagination and limited creative thinking.
3. Slow reaction time.
4. Apathy, diffidence, dependence, placidity—but frequent presence of excitability, sensitivity.
5. Academic retardation, especially in reading; achievement age lagging behind chronological age.
6. Absence or easy loss of self-confidence.
7. Gullibility, instability, shyness, submissiveness.
8. Low power of retention and memory.
9. Inability to do abstract thinking, to handle symbols, to evaluate results, to foresee consequences of acts.
10. Failure to transfer ideas, to extend beyond local point of view in time or place, to retain interest if results are deferred or intangible.
11. Limited powers of self-direction, of adapting to change in situations and people.
12. Low levels of initiative, vocabulary, standards of workmanship, persistence, concentration, reasoning, defining, discriminating, analyzing.
13. Ease of confusion; fears, anxieties.
14. Laziness—but perhaps due to ill health or emotional maladjustment rather than as a constitutional factor.
15. Action based on impulse; insistence on quick results; inclination toward jumping to conclusions.
16. Less well-developed physically—height, weight, proportion, general health, unexplained fatigue.

An important area of characteristics relates to developments in early childhood. Delay in sitting up, walking, and talking may be indications of slow development, but some who are average or even bright are also late in these abilities. A list of typical behavior patterns, if used objectively and selectively, is sometimes of value to parents for comparison purposes.[3] Help is sometimes needed from those who can be more objective than parents usually are.

---

[3] Samuel A. Kirk, Merle B. Karnes, and Winifred D. Kirk, *You and Your Retarded Child* (New York: The Macmillan Company, 1955), pp. 14–28.

Because of a child's special gifts or talents, teachers may also be misled into believing a child is brighter than he really is. Equally misleading can be particularly attractive personalities, reasonably high achievement in one or more academic areas, or leadership in athletic or other activities. The teacher cannot assume that all who do the following are slow learners, even though many of them are: ask questions, frequently of irrelevant nature; demand attention; withdraw from academic work; withdraw from social situations into either shy or aggressive framework; cheat, argue, or create other disciplinary situations.

Another aspect of problems related to some of these children is evident in comments like the following: "Problems of truancy, delinquency, behavior, and disinterest in school work are more frequent with this group than with average or superior children. Surveys made on populations of correctional institutions or 'reform schools' have invariably shown that the majority of children in such institutions are dull-normal and backward, with I.Q.'s ranging from 75 to 90." [4]

Identification Techniques

Three factors are of special importance at the outset in considering how to identify slow learners: (1) the identification process should begin early; (2) no single index or device is sufficient; and (3) the process should continue over a relatively long period of time. If the child advances at a slower rate than normal for a number of years, a slight deviation at the age of three or four may result in a more severe deviation at a later time. Because early identification of slowness might be especially misleading, however, it may be necessary to reserve judgment and to follow up in greater detail and with increasingly refined instruments.

One of the by-products of our increased birth rate has been the parents' tendency to send children to school at an earlier age and also to keep children in school for a longer period of time. School enrollment figures from the Bureau of Census in 1959 indicated that 97 per cent of all six-year-old children and 64 per cent of all

[4] Samuel A. Kirk, *Teaching Reading to Slow-Learning Children* (New York: Houghton Mifflin Company, 1940), p. 174.

the five-year-olds were in school.[5] The number of four- and three-year-olds in nurseries or play-schools is also increasing.[6] On the basis of preschool health examinations, parent-teacher conferences, and legal provisions which make early treatment and related services possible, there will not only be fewer children in the special education classes, but the special education classes can more adequately serve the needs of the children who will be enrolled.[7] Ingram emphasizes the importance of early understanding of individual patterns of growth and says, ". . . it is desirable that all slow-learning children be recognized at an early age and be provided with suitable educational opportunities from the beginning. Such a program could reasonably be expected to increase greatly the number of individuals with good habits, healthy attitudes, self-confidence, and self-reliance to carry on to the limit of their ability in the home, the school, and the community." [8]

Jewett and Hull describe the four items used in discovering or identifying rapid- and slow-learning pupils: teachers' marks, group intelligence tests, teachers' estimates of school achievement, and standardized achievement tests. Use of these techniques usually provides quantitative data for grouping pupils. Their report includes some differences in practice between the small and large high schools. Large high schools report more extensive use of individual intelligence tests, anecdotal reports, and guidance counselors. In both large and small high schools, parents were seldom consulted for the purpose of discovering either a rapid or a slow learner.[9]

Modern tests and testing procedures have greatly contributed to our understanding of individual differences and to the extent and size of such differences. Intelligence, aptitude, and achievement tests and the various measurements of personality have yielded certain scores, but too often have not been interpreted to yield further diagnostic information. Too often teachers who are subject-centered

---

[5] James L. Taylor, Lillian L. Gore, and Hazel F. Gabbard, *Functional Schools for Young Children*, U.S. Department of Health, Education, and Welfare No. OE-21006, Special Publication No. 8, 1961, p. 1.

[6] *Ibid.*, p. 3.

[7] Cruickshank and Johnson, *op. cit.*, p. 97.

[8] Ingram, *op. cit.*, p. 105.

[9] Arno Jewett and J. Dan Hull, Coordinators, *Teaching Rapid and Slow Learners in High Schools*, U.S. Department of Health, Education, and Welfare Bulletin No. 5, 1954.

consider test items in terms of the course of study. They become more concerned with a score than with evidence revealed by performance on individual items—evidence which may indicate needed changes in the curriculum or increased individual guidance in learning. Evaluation needs to be concerned with growth of the total personality. Teachers need to maintain questioning attitudes which help to identify causes of behavior. Identification techniques have as their chief function to find out how the child is growing and developing, including a major reference to the child's former status. Part of the job involves a closer relationship between the home and the school.[10]

McClelland and Baldwin in *Talent and Society* discuss the "lack of fit" between performance in school and that in later life, and speak of this problem particularly in relation to the child who may be a "late bloomer." The error is in assuming that the school and life require identical abilities or characteristic traits. More needs to be known about the constancy of various traits in the personality over a period of time and about the particular ways in which these traits develop throughout childhood. There is a need to analyze the functional characteristics of various performance situations, including the school, the professions, and various occupations, so that better predictions can be made by uncovering functional identities.[11]

Among the kinds of information desired are the following: physical, emotional, and mental development; defects and/or deviations from the normal; abilities, interests, achievement; family and community background; school data. Included in these areas of information should be specific details related to speech development, motor ability, vocabulary growth, and personality factors. The most widely used identification *techniques and materials* are these:

1. Individual intelligence tests.
2. Group intelligence tests.
3. Personality tests.
4. Sociometric techniques to measure relationships among specific children in groups.

[10] Helen Heffernan, "Evaluation—More Than Testing," reprinted in Victor H. Noll and Rachel P. Noll, *Readings in Educational Psychology* (New York: The Macmillan Company, 1962), pp. 497–502.
[11] D. C. McClelland, *et al., Talent and Society* (Princeton, N.J.: D. Van Nostrand Co., Inc., 1958).

5. Achievement tests to measure subject-matter accomplishment.

6. Physical examinations to study growth and to discern defects.

7. Home and community information, based on forms filled out by parents, school social worker, and other professional personnel; use of home interviews and family history forms.

8. Anecdotal records objectively selected and prepared, based on teacher observations regarding the child.

9. Teacher judgments regarding achievement and personality.

10. Child interviews; other information from guidance counselors.

11. School history form which may include achievement test scores, grades, and other information listed above.

12. Teacher-prepared materials; tests and games related to information and memory.[12]

The organization and interpretation of such data may be made according to any one of the suggested frameworks available in the literature discussing child study techniques (Prescott,[13] Driscoll,[14] White [15]). Prescott suggests the following steps as being essential in the interpretation of such data:

1. Arrange the facts in accord with an organizing framework of information.

2. Check the facts. Ferret out contradictions and areas needing further study and information.

3. Look for clues that will uncover blind spots, such as when information is too scanty, or where prejudices are involved.

4. Identify and list recurring situations and patterns of behavior.

5. Spot significant unique events.

6. Form a series of hypotheses to account for particular patterns of behavior.

7. Relate the hypotheses about different patterns of behavior to each other, to form an understanding of the child's total personality.

---

[12] Various child study forms or adaptations of them provide for the accumulation of this kind of information. For example, Willard Abraham, *A New Look at Reading* (Boston: Porter Sargent, 1956), pp. 95–116. Four forms: Parents, Health, School, Child.

[13] American Council on Education, *Helping Teachers Understand Children* (Washington, D.C.: The Council, 1945).

[14] Gertrude Driscoll, *How To Study the Behavior of Children* (New York: Bureau of Publications, Teachers College, Columbia University, 1941).

[15] Verna White, *Studying the Individual Pupil* (New York: Harper & Row, Publishers, 1958).

8. Check the hypotheses against the complete information, to discover contradictions, over-simplifications, biased interpretations.

9. Plan practical ways that might make a helpful program for this child.

10. Evaluate the hypotheses in relation to observed changes as a result of using certain programs which grew out of #9 above.[16]

A number of specific suggestions related to the many identification procedures can be made: Use the mental age rather than the intelligence quotient so that the level at which the child can work might be more definitely determined; discern whether his being overage in grade is because of nonpromotion or because of a late start in school; recognize that individual testing (despite its value as an integral part of the identification process) is expensive and time-consuming, and measure its value against other techniques if a choice must be made; study the physical, intelligence, and scholastic records for stability and consistency; study the specific parts of tests rather than only consolidated test scores; evaluate relationships between achievement and intelligence; note and interpret the effects of home and family information, such as mobility, divorce, death, and sickness; realize that achievement as an identification factor is inconclusive, because the hard-working slow child may perform more adequately than the careless brighter one.

In the past, many slow children have gone through our schools and into the working world without having in any way been identified. In some instances identification could have had a detrimental effect, calling special attention to an individual who is close to the normal and capable of adjusting to home, community, and occupational settings in a manner that satisfies both him and society. There are too many cases of maladjustment, however, and knowledge of these children, identification procedures, and program adaptations cannot be left to chance.

Attitudes, Interests, and Ambitions of Slow Learners

Although some attention has already been paid to the attitudes and interests of slow learners, a few of the more commonly recognized ones should be noted in more detail. Because of neglect and

---

[16] American Council on Education, *op. cit.*, pp. 185–94.

frequent failure to adapt school programs to their needs, a puzzled state of mind and feelings of inferiority may develop. The usual anticipation of young children toward school may change to indifference and then to resentment. Slow learners face many of the same pressures as the normal children but exhibit an inability to cope with them. Frustration may develop into compensatory reactions, attention-getting devices, or stubborn nonconformity. Large children in the same little chairs for two, three, or four years will seldom retain the original happy outlook toward school, family, playmates, and life in general that is usually observed in normal children. The feeling of being left out or left back may have cumulative effects.

The interests of slow learners as demonstrated by hobbies, school activities, reading choices, and feelings about school subjects vary from those of average children. High school slow learners list collecting as the favorite of a very limited number of hobbies in which they engage. Sports and athletics, club and committee work, and musical activities are among the school activities most frequently selected. Their reading interests are toward the easy-to-read magazines (western, detective, mystery, movie). The most liked high school subject is shop; the least liked, English. Knowledge of world affairs is very low. The need for guidance is obvious in all of these areas.[17]

Although more of the bright than slow high school students intend to go to college, the latter frequently display excessively high ambitions, often stimulated by parents.[18] The inappropriateness of the ambitions indicates the need for child and parent guidance toward a realistic appraisal of abilities and potential, in order to avoid later frustration and dissension.

Basic Needs

There are more similarities than differences between the needs of slow learners and others. They, too, need a balance between success

---

[17] Glenn Myers Blair, *Mentally Superior and Inferior Children in the Junior and Senior High School* (New York: Bureau of Publications, Teachers College, Columbia University, 1938).
[18] *Ibid.*

and failure, physical well-being, recognition of abilities and problems, measurement of progress in terms of capacity, and the help
that all children need in establishing worthwhile, realistic goals.
They, too, need affection, acceptance, and achievement. As with
other children, their needs and the ways to satisfy them must be
individualized as much as possible, within the limitations of a particular family, school, and community.

> The sub-normal child, like the normal child, is a unique per-
> sonality, having physiological drives, instincts and emotions which
> crave satisfaction; intellectual abilities, social potentialities, and the
> capacity to acquire modes of behavior, interests, attitudes and skills.
> All of these must be developed and integrated. At each level of
> intelligence, however, from the normal to the defective, the vitality
> of these components of personality becomes weaker. This weakness
> is most noticeable in the intellectual skills, in the capacity for ab-
> stract thought and reasoning, in the power of controlling impulses
> and of adjusting to new circumstances. It is least noticeable on the
> level of instinct and emotional impulse . . .[19]

Although the needs of normal and sub-normal children may be
similar, differences exist in degree and emphasis. The following
should be taken into account: academic work, but more concrete,
realistic, meaningful; planning, but shorter range; relating words,
ideas, learnings, but on simpler, more repetitive level; help and
stimulation, but more frequently provided; activities, but of a more
nonverbal nature.

The hierarchical nature of human needs evolves into the following basic ideas:

1. Objects and persons to satisfy inner physiological needs.
   a. Food to satisfy hunger.
   b. Drink to satisfy thirst.
   c. Sex objects to satisfy sex cravings.
2. Safety—the need to escape from outer dangers.
3. Acceptance—affection, love, affiliation, belonging, compan-
ionship, friendship.
4. Approval, prestige, status.
5. Self-esteem, self-respect, self-satisfaction.
6. Mastery, success, achievement.
7. Independence.

---

[19] Frances Lloyd, *Educating the Sub-Normal Child* (New York: Philosophical
Library, 1953), p. 7.

The higher goals cannot be reached when the individual is still struggling to satisfy more basic needs.[20] If the public school teacher is the only professional person who will serve the needs of many public school children, then her need for knowledge about the growth process and developmental levels is surely a basic tool. The child who is hungry, controlled by fears, or rejected may not have a coping mechanism strong enough to make it possible for him to respond to the teacher.

All children face problems, but because slow learners are less able to solve them, the obstacles take on greater proportions. It is necessary for parents and teachers to recognize that what may be an easily solved task for an average child might bring out difficult behavior from the slow learner merely because they fail to anticipate the pending frustration.

Basic Goals

Goals for all children, in school and later on in life, have frequently been stated in pedantic terms rather than in this brief manner: good health, mental and physical; mastery of knowledge and critical thinking up to capacity; vocational preparation and adjustment; skill in human relationships—family, society; personal development, based on abilities, aptitudes, and interests.

For slow learners, adaptations must be made in these objectives for "... the goals of learning must be discernible, obvious and reasonably immediate" for them.[21] These adaptations are related to factors such as the following, which represent a realistic approach to these children:

1. They cannot achieve as many and as varied adjustments as normal children.
2. They cannot contribute to or participate in life as fully as normal children.
3. They can achieve adjustment within their reach.

[20] Percival M. Symonds, *What Education Has to Learn From Psychology* (New York: Bureau of Publications, Teachers College, Columbia University, 1958), p. 6.
[21] B. L. Dodds, "What Is a Good Program for the Slow Learner?" *Bulletin of the National Association of Secondary-School Principals,* Vol. 36, No. 185 (March, 1952), p. 331.

4. They can contribute their share to accomplishing the tasks of life.

5. They can enjoy life at their own level of interest and accomplishment.

6. They cannot be expected to understand the complexities of the social order or to contribute to the solution of its problems.

7. They will be followers.

8. Their mental development will be slow.

9. Average standards will more easily be attained in physical and social development than in mental development.

10. Home environments often provide inadequate opportunities for experience.

11. Hand skills are the sphere of greatest likely success.

12. Adjustments must ultimately be made chiefly in the ranks of semiskilled and unskilled occupations.[22]

There is a basic and close relationship between the goals and needs of the slow learners, and it is vital that they participate in the establishment of the former and an understanding of the latter.

Multihandicaps

Just as normal or bright children may have overlapping abilities, slow learners may have disabilities that are interrelated. Sometimes they become confused in the cause-and-effect relationship. For example, a limited demonstration of intelligence may result from handicaps in sight, hearing, and emotional adjustment and in speech or orthopedic difficulties. Or, limited intelligence may itself result in emotional maladjustment.

A selective use of identification techniques and materials will help determine the areas for concern and their interrelationship. The emphasis in this analysis will have to be on degree. The existence of more than one handicap may, of course, complicate what might seem to be a well-defined difficulty, but the basic problem of working with children or others toward a realistic solution of their problems is always present. The teacher's task is made greater because he does not have the controls of a scientific laboratory situation. Perhaps therein lies its fascination and appeal for the social scientist, the teacher, and the parent.

---

[22] Ingram, *op. cit.*, pp. 62–72.

Another Kind of Slow Learner

Practically all the professional literature on slow learners is devoted to the children as defined earlier—those with an intelligence range of approximately 75 to 90 I.Q., or those performing at that level despite indications of higher capabilities. However, there is a significant number of children whose educational neglect has been great, whose potentialities as contributing members of a democratic society are strong, and who literally are "slow learners." They are the bright children working below their considerable capacities and learning more slowly than they are capable of doing. They are the undermotivated, underachieving students who tragically add to our educational drop-out rate, the ones whom some schools overlook when they attempt to set up programs for gifted children who are able and ambitious. Ability is there, but the ambition may be limited or lacking.

In guiding children we recognize the need for a coordination of ability, achievement, and aspiration. With slow learners of the type to which most of this monograph is devoted and with mentally retarded children lower on the intellectual scale, the ability and achievement factors are invariably limited. But with the category of "slow learner" discussed here the situation is different: ability is high; achievement is lower; and aspiration as it relates to the educational and vocational future may or may not be high.

These children may be in fifth grade, for example, operating satisfactorily at that level, but their ability could carry them higher. The unfortunate part is that they, their teachers, and perhaps even their parents may be satisfied with their performance. Many of the writings of Terman, Hollingworth, and others have stressed this problem. Their concern is shown in statements like these:

> One-third to one-half of the "top" high school graduates do not complete college; these may add up to 500,000 or more students each year.
> Children with I.Q.'s of 140 waste half their time in the ordinary elementary school situation; those above 170 I.Q. waste practically all of their time.
> More than half of the children with I.Q.'s of 135 or above have mastered the school curriculum to a point two or more full grades beyond the one in which they are enrolled.

A tragic loss occurs because the gifted ones may not be recognized and are permitted to slip through as mediocrities.

Riessman discusses the "slow gifted child" who is culturally deprived and who is categorized as "slow." There is need to realize that slowness in learning can reflect many things.[23] Various approaches can be made to a basic discussion of the gifted "slow learners." They can be looked at, for example, from the viewpoint of the labor market. In recent years we have read many times of our country's increasing need for skilled and professional personnel. The relatively high drop-out rate and underachievement of many of our bright children decrease the possibility of meeting those needs in the years ahead. If the viewpoint of leadership is used, we may be concerned because thousands of our potential leaders fail to achieve to their capacities; they are learning less and more slowly than their abilities indicate they could.

Another approach is through the problem of the high drop-out rate of these potentially promising young people, a problem that can be traced to many sources. School records, questionnaires, and interviews in depth may give different reasons from the same child. In general, they revolve around finances, poor teaching, lack of guidance, or low parental and/or community aspiration levels. They may occur early with the drop-out itself actually being only the culmination, the result of the accumulation of trivialities dating back many years. The evidence in drop-out studies shows that it is imperative to identify potential drop-outs as soon as symptoms of failure and discouragement are known in the child's school career. This would mean increased liaison between elementary, secondary, and college levels. It would mean beginning with the first grader who experiences failure.[24] The situation has sometimes been compared with divorce, which may come about through the same kind of cumulative process.

The key word for many of the gifted "slow learners" is "motivation." Are they motivated sufficiently to perform to their capacities? The answer obviously must be, "No." Then, if they are not, what

[23] Frank Riessman, *The Culturally Deprived Child* (New York: Harper & Row, Publishers, 1962), p. 64.

[24] Stanley E. Hecker, *Early School Leavers in Kentucky,* Bulletin of the Bureau of School Service, College of Education, University of Kentucky, Vol. XXV, No. 4 (June, 1953).

can be done about them? This difficult question can be stated in another way: How does a teacher, school, home, or community help or encourage a bright child to learn when he has all sorts of reasons—real or imagined—for not doing so? It is with that question that the following section is concerned.

Motivation of the Gifted "Slow Learner"

The underachievement of many gifted children is serious. Working with the problem is neither easy nor inexpensive. It is a detailed, difficult, costly process, but well worth the effort. The choice is a relatively simple one to express: Do it, and help meet society's major ills with the skilled personnel capable of working toward those goals; ignore it, and delay solution of society's medical, social, and other problems; lose the major contributions of potentially qualified personnel, and condone the frustrations of many who for their entire lives operate on a plane below their own capabilities.

The symptoms of poor study habits, the pattern of underachievement, the frequency of boys more than girls in the underachiever category, the overlapping reasons (such as broken and disturbed homes, poor physical health, family mobility, parental rejection, immaturity and others)—all lead to a framework for listing some recommendations and ideas to help solve the problem of lack of motivation or existence of underachievement. The ten items that follow dig deeply into the issue:

The causes behind the problem. A child who has difficulty with reading will not necessarily have his problems solved by giving him more to read. The cause must be discovered and removed, or at least altered. So it is with the underachievers. What is it that interferes with their learning? Directly involved in this question and in its answer are the techniques of child study. Included among them are testing (achievement, intelligence), anecdotal records, observation, sociometry, play therapy, paintings, and other materials prepared by the children. Full case studies are also used. The qualifications of the persons administering these materials and interpreting them must not, of course, be left to chance.

Persons who can help. It has become almost a cliché to refer to something as a "team effort," for when a team, group, or committee is involved, the responsibility may be shifted so often that it becomes lost. When the problem of a child is concerned, however, there is the need for a multiple approach. The difficulty in both the causation and solution of the problem may be so involved that a unilateral approach by even the best-intentioned person may not result in a satisfying conclusion. Conspicuously present in the picture are the following (and there certainly may be others, depending upon the individual child involved):

Parents.   Despite their own pressures of family conflicts, lack of money, and other difficulties, parents are able to provide information available from no other source. Their subjectivity can be discounted in skilled hands which dig professionally into those facts of environment that can add to knowledge available through other techniques. The example they provide (or that they *can* provide if guided healthfully to do so), the assumptions they have made and perhaps acted upon, the authoritative confusion to which they have been subjected from professional and pseudoprofessional writers and speakers—all can be helpful in the broad framework of resources available to help a particular child perform in line with his capacity.

Teachers.   Teaching large numbers of children, occasionally feeling threatened by children brighter than they are, and working under a heavy work load, teachers can still be of help by what they know about specific children. Their awareness of knowledge may be limited by what they read, how they feel about bright children, what their attitude is toward education as a whole and scholarly areas in particular, what example they set; but they still are the persons closest to the academic life of children and therefore know most about their deficiencies and abilities as far as the academic environment is concerned.

Children.   The values, culture, attitudes, and abilities of children can all be studied and analyzed. What do the children indicate about their growth and development, about the reasons for the kind of limitations in them? How much can we find out from what children say, do, write, or think? These criteria, too, are sources for insight and bases for action that may lead to achievement and aspiration. The peer group may ridicule the bilingual child who tenaciously continues his education, even though all indications point to merely delayed employment at the plant or factory where members of the peer group are already employed. This kind of problem as it exists in the hopes and dreams of our gifted children must be seen in its proper perspective. What it tells us about the motivation of the gifted "slow learner" may be significant.

The place of inspiration. The child who is bright and fast, but who moves at a slow pace academically, needs outside interest, enthusiasm, and support. Though some may consider this point to be naïve or unrealistic, it must be stated and recognized for its real worth: The key to unlock a push toward achievement commensurate with one's abilities may come from the inspiration provided by one adult for a child. This one-to-one relationship, whether it comes from a teacher, guidance person, parent, school administrator, neighbor, or sibling may provide the one bit of stimulation that has been missing. This may be the needed segment toward helping the child realize he is important or smart or capable. Such inspiration may be expensive (if provided by a professional person working with many young people), but the American dream of educating all children to their capacities is costly as well as worthy. Few thoughtful people could conclude otherwise.

"Taking the child where he is." Terminology in the field of education is frequently rather vague, indecisive, and indirect. Too often phrases such as "individual differences," "educating all children to their capacities," and "the whole child" have been used without the specificity needed for their full understanding and implementation. The area of exceptional children—where identification, teaching techniques, educational materials, and class and school organization are almost forced to become detailed and specific—provides one of the few parts of the education framework where indefinite approaches are not acceptable. A realistic appraisal that recognizes where the gifted "slow learner" is in his personal and academic development may help point the way toward his reaching goals of which he is capable. The teacher and counselor involved in that process may thus be able to motivate him on the basis of the factual knowledge they have about him.

A time for an "earthy approach." What encourages us to battle the problems of overweight, a faulty golf game, making ends meet financially, or playing bridge better than the neighbors with whom we've been competing for years? The stimulant varies from one problem to another, and from one individual to another. Although the sheer enjoyment of reading, solving problems, or performing scientific experiments may provide the motivation that helps some bright children perform to their capacities, for others a more basic (and some will insist, a less desirable) approach can be successful. It is a matter for one to decide whether the end is worth the means employed. For example:

Earnings. Figures have been used many times which indicate that the lifetime earnings of the average college graduate is $100,-000 or more in excess of the average high school graduate.

Grades. It is not enough to place bright youngsters in "honors" or other special class settings and hope that such placement will be sufficient motivation for all of them. To expect an "A" or its equivalent in a special class to mean the same thing as an "A" in a regular class assumes that grades have lost the meaning which has unfortunately been so strongly attached to them for many years. Successful methods have been used in numerous school systems to weight the grades so that on the transcript a heavier credit is recognized for similar grades obtained in special classes or courses. Another approach has been to assure the student of a top grade as long as he performs adequately in the enriched setting. A third approach is to footnote the type of class on transcripts so that colleges and universities to which they are sent can recognize the distinction.

Guidance in terms of change. When it comes to vocations of the present and future, the status quo is bound to be wrong. Although the U.S. Bureau of Labor Statistics and other public, professional, and private sources can be helpful, no one can be sure what tomorrow will bring in occupational changes, despite the existence of trends expertly analyzed. For this point to take on real meaning, all we need ask is this: How much did we know 20 or 25 years ago about the tremendous recent changes and demands of science, engineering, and even the field of teaching? We cannot now know with certainty which fields will be in short supply that far in advance—or, in fact (on the basis of recent experiences), what new fields will exist of which we at present are not even aware. One of the world's oldest religions has as one of its statements the admonition to "limit not thy children to thine own ideas. They are born in a different time."

Honors classes. Special classes for qualified students, who may or may not be working up to their capacities, have already been mentioned as they relate to grading methods. Some students are deliberately holding back in order to be part of the acceptable majority. In some settings it may not be fashionable either to work hard or to get good grades, and the awareness of this fact by school administrators and their teachers and guidance personnel is essential. The existence of special classes and their development as settings for challenging learning experiences can sometimes help students who operate at a pace slower and lower than their aptitudes indicate they should.

The factor of freedom. Although the attitudes toward bright children are based on freedom, acceptance, and understanding problems and are a matter of degree and of relationship, too often in recent years many people have loaded burdens on children in direct proportion to their ability to learn. This approach implies a double standard—one for children and another for adults: for one, a longer school day and school year, less television watching, and more homework; for the other, a shorter work day and work year, as much television watching as desired, and more freedom for leisure activities. Such inconsistencies result in various reactions on the part of some of the young people, including a penetrating evaluation of the educational activities to which they are exposed, with the inevitable conclusion that some of them are found to be lacking in purpose. A recent educational film on gifted children arrives at the mistaken conclusion that a ten-year-old with an I.Q. of 130 thinks and acts like a thirteen-year-old; a ten-year-old with an I.Q. of 170 or 180 thinks and acts like a seventeen- or eighteen-year-old, and one with an I.Q. of 200 thinks and acts like a person 20 years old. Such interpretations interfere with a child who happens to be bright and who is enjoying the one childhood he is entitled to. Such interference can slow the learning process for him, because expectations and pressures may be all wrong. If there is any time appropriate for having fun, being different, exercising creativity, and experimenting with knowledge and life, the childhood years are that time. To treat intellect with a heavy burden of seriousness may stifle or discourage its normal growth.

A fallacy of the highest academic degree. Sometimes we assume slowness exists because of lack of enthusiasm toward the highest levels of education. To attempt to motivate bright young people toward goals of that type may be totally fallacious; the goals may be entirely out of line with their real aims. We err, for example, if we feel that the brightest must obtain the top academic degrees. In the fields of engineering and business, especially, it may be that such academic accomplishments may be unnecessary for the most capable and most creative; for them an educational aim one or two steps below the very top may be the most effective background for their own competent performance. Those who need the topmost degrees behind their names may be using them as security and a step toward advancement, a need not felt by the more creative individuals who recognize that their own abilities combined with a more limited formal education may help them reach vocational goals with greater ease and satisfaction. If we judge by the pedantic demands of various standardized intelligence tests, the creative individuals may appear to be slow, but it is the tests that may be in error as they fail to measure some of the less discernible factors of intelligence.

Motivation related to deprivation. In order to motivate the gifted "slow learner," deprivation may be one of the most unusual and most effective techniques available. The idea may have little attraction in this era when it is assumed that all children profit from an environment based on enrichment and success at every turn. Is that really true for all children? A session of professional psychologists and educators recently chose the theme of the education of gifted children. "If we could have the most ideal circumstances, materials, and teaching," they asked themselves, "what would we want for bright children?" The accumulated list was lengthy, expensive, and ideal. But then they wondered: "Would this environment oppress and suffocate the talents these children have? How would Van Gogh and others like him perform? Is there a possibility that their contributions would be limited by the abundance they would find on all sides?"

Basic psychological terminology. To reach the child himself, it is necessary to dig incisively through the terms that attempt to describe problems of children. Over-protective, dominant, aggressive, shy, Oedipus complex—the tags frequently interfere with a full understanding of what the child is really like, what made him that way, and what may be done about it. They may perpetuate his slower pace merely because they serve as a cover for more basic difficulties and identify symptoms rather than real causes, and with varying degrees of accuracy at that. Educational films which describe two-year-olds as "terrible," four-year-olds as "frustrating," and adolescents as in "turmoil" may be accurate in many cases, but they may provide convenient handles that fail to determine or uncover far more serious factors beneath the surface.

Early identification. One of the most important items related to motivating gifted "slow learners" is that they must be discerned early, because otherwise the habits of mediocrity may be established beyond repair. Secondary schools should not wait for them to enroll before they are identified. Why should the high schools not cooperate closely with the elementary schools in records, program, and materials? And if such cooperation is effective, should it not continue down through the grades into the primary level, kindergarten, and nursery school? The indications of brightness stand out early through vocabulary, performance, and other signs. To ignore them is to encourage slovenly academic habits and slower rates of progress than the levels toward which early intelligence points. Easier than correcting the problems of these "slow learners" as they progress in school is the prevention of the problems. This can be done by noting and beginning to act on the children's brightness in the early years.

The preceding approaches and ideas related to the motivation and underachievement of this category of "slow learner" brings up the need for an individualized approach to the lag in their growth and learning. From an unusual source (Danny Kaye) comes the statement, "You can't bring health and happiness to a million children by signing a paper or waving a wand. It has to be done child by child." To health and happiness might be added "achievement."

In addition to thinking through (and acting upon) appropriate sections of the ten guidelines already indicated, teachers may want to bring the problem of motivating these able, but underperforming, children closer to their own classrooms by asking themselves the following questions:

1. What is the best teaching I've ever seen, heard about, or read about? What techniques, materials, and attitudes seemed to work best?

2. What is the best teaching I've ever done or of which I am capable?

3. When have the children been most excited in the learning process, most curious, critical and doubting, most eager to use encyclopedias and other library materials, most oblivious to ends of class periods?

The answers to these questions may indicate limits which many teachers have not yet reached and heights of achievement on their own part not yet sought. Variations of these questions, with similar objectives in mind, may be asked by school administrators and parents.

CHAPTER III

The Parents and the Community

The first, most concerned, and most important teacher is the parent, the most involved adult of all in the development and education of the slow learner. People usually agree when discussing parental responsibilities, the vitality of the parents' contribution toward their children's education, and their involvement in either the speed or the slowness of a child's advances. Psychologists stress the importance of parents when they write of the influences of early environment and the negative effects of parental disharmony, neglect, or rejection.

Problems of Parents and the Slow Learner

Whether one talks of the slow learner whose limitations are to be accepted or of the one whose mental processes can be elevated considerably when the causes which shackle the processes are identified and eliminated, the attitudes of parents have a strong influence on the education and adjustment of the child. The feelings and relationships may be complicated and inextricably involved with the concept the parent has of himself, as well as with his inability to evaluate the child's potential objectively.

A child whose progress is slow may be seen as a threat or insult, with injustices accruing to the child or his school. His slowness may also be denied or ignored. Another reaction may be that of disguised rejection demonstrated by oversolicitous or hostile attitudes. The actions of the parents—or the feelings, words, or ideas never completely submerged or hidden from a child made sensitive to them—will affect the home relationships and the school work of that child. Excessive daydreaming, withdrawal, temper tantrums, or other examples of antisocial behavior may evolve.

Resentment and misunderstanding demand elimination in most of our relationships with children, but they are sometimes especially persistent in clinging to the parents of children most in need of acceptance and full understanding. The education cliché of "taking the child where he is" applies with great force to the parent of a slow learner. To see abilities and limitations as they are, to accept characteristics that are not always lovable, to respect achievement which is even less than mediocre by artificial standards but is high for this child, to dislike what is done but never to reject the child— these are tests for parents of slow learners to pass, tests that try their patience, character, and love. But the importance of passing them is great, for children are seldom deceived about our basic attitudes toward them.

Parents who recognize that these children have the same basic needs as other children know that satisfaction in accomplishment is a relative thing. A bright child harnesses a tricky gas in a laboratory experiment, and we are proud of him. But pride can also come in a slow learner's reading skill when our expectations are very low, or even in a far more severely retarded child's learning to drink through a straw when all hope seems to be lost.

Brighter brothers and sisters, high (and unrealistic) vocational aspirations, and competitive grading systems all constitute threats to the child's adjustments and the parents' acceptance of him. The escapades of normal adolescents are far less of a strain on family cohesion than is the slowly emerging truth that the cherished first born not only won't become a doctor, but he may not even finish high school. Although expectations may be low or limited, they can be honest and based on the pride which all children need for self-respect.

Protection from the "harsh world" may be another parental error. It may be based on unwarranted praise, too much help, too much watching and concern. It is difficult sometimes to realize that a child who thinks slowly *can* think, and one whose sensitivity arouses slowly *can* have it aroused. Problems of this kind are a family responsibility. Teachers, administrators, guidance personnel, and others can help and can provide some understanding, but the basic concern remains where it starts. The first answers to questions, the first adjustment of toys and books to abilities, and the first acceptance of limitations are given at home where the pace is set for what the school will do later.

A generation ago the young mother was guided by her mother and her grandmother in utilizing child-rearing operations, which were tested by practice and believed to be true. Changed styles in family patterns and different cultural mores more often today result in a young mother's knowledge that the one thing she will not do with her child is to repeat the practices her mother used with her. New knowledge about child growth and development is often not readily available to the families who have the greatest need for understanding and knowing what should be expected of a child. Parent education classes sponsored by some school systems through adult education programs have been effective in meeting this need in some parts of the country.[1]

Links between school and parent are strong in any case, but especially so where slow learners are involved. Because their parents have faced so many failures even before the first day the child is in school, they are frequently especially eager for reports—and they hope so strongly that the reports are of progress. Whether they are or not, the parents want to know, and they need all the help the school can give in explaining differences and limitations in abilities and in plans for meeting individual differences. Although the reports should put emphasis on the positive, they must be honest.

Parents are often trapped in the overwhelming and vicious circle which began with their own culturally deprived and educationally impoverished background. The school has traditionally been rather unsympathetic toward this parent. The typically middle-class value system of school personnel has become a stereotype that has accepted surface evidence that the parents are not interested in the child's school or subsequent education. PTA meetings are notoriously poorly attended in neighborhoods of minority groups or in low socio-economic areas.

But what has the school traditionally held out to these parents as a basis upon which much needed home-school cooperation could be based? The Higher Horizons program has effectively demonstrated that parents from such neighborhoods (who have previously been hostile to and alienated from the school) have achieved spectacular changes in their own communities when genuine motivation

---

[1] Katherine Whiteside Taylor, "A Community-Wide Program of Parent Education," *Children*, Vol. 9, No. 1 (January-February, 1962), pp. 9–14.

was present. Dr. John H. Niemeyer referred to the potential learning ability of the alienated families and their children as "the social atom," the splitting of which could release for society tremendous forces for good.[2] Initially called The Demonstration Guidance Project, The Higher Horizon's program started in 1956 at Junior High School No. 43 in New York City. Its success has spread to 13 major cities under the sponsorship of the Ford Foundation's "Great Cities School Improvement Program."

In these programs, parents have been included. Daytime meetings were held with parents on all grade levels for the purpose of acquainting them with the program and to gain cooperation. Evening meetings were arranged for parents who could not attend in the day. When parents could attend neither meeting, home visits were made by the social case worker. Letters explaining new steps or special features in the program were sent to parents. Workshops were organized to give parents opportunties to discuss career possibilities for their children.

Counseling techniques were useful to gain specific home cooperation in such ways as control of television time or use of private study space. Parents demonstrated their desire to cooperate when they understood what to do and when their own problems were handled with understanding and acceptance. Frank Riessman raises basic questions regarding the school's need for working with and for better understanding the different value-system and life goals among people of culturally deprived environments.[3]

For slow learners, even more than for other children, the conference method is more satisfying than a report card based on numbers and symbols. What the child has demonstrated in scholastic ability should be discussed in these conferences, but they also should include details related to physical condition, emotional stability, academic growth, and the qualities of cooperation, initiative, social adjustment, self-direction, and self-evaluation.

Parent-teacher conferences can be a time when the people most familiar with the child can pool information and arrive at a mutual

---

[2] John H. Niemeyer, "Splitting the Social Atom," *Saturday Review* (September 12, 1959).

[3] Riessman, *op. cit.*, pp. 107–11.

understanding of goals and directions. Langdon and Stout,[4] D'Evelyn,[5] Strang,[6] and Prescott [7] are among the authors whose suggestions for conferences include useful guides and techniques. Parents see a child in several ways: what they hope he is; what they fear he may be; what they think he really is; what they think others think of him; and what they hoped he would be. It is well to remember this projection, which often involves a description of the ideal child. Also, the child's role of behavior may for various reasons be different in the school from what it is in the home. Teacher training has traditionally not included an opportunity for teachers to learn conference techniques or gain experience in understanding the dynamics involved.

Social, intellectual, and emotional worlds of parents and teachers may be sufficiently different to make communication between some personalities difficult. Driscoll in *How to Study the Behavior of Children* suggests the following criteria in planning for parent conferences:

> 1. One in which parents and teacher are doing about the same amount of "telling."
> 2. One in which the parent sees that the teacher thoroughly enjoys the interesting behavior of her child.
> 3. One in which the teacher is able to approve of some attitude or method that the parent is using.
> 4. One in which the parent becomes more relaxed as the conference continues.[8]

Parents want specific techniques and ways through which they can assist their child in making maximum use of his ability. Interpreting simple procedures in steps of learning is a guideline to parents who have never considered their own role in teaching their children. They need help in understanding that the slow-learning

---

[4] Grace Langdon and Irving W. Stout, *Parent-Teacher Relationships,* Research Bulletin 16 (Washington, D.C.: American Educational Research Association, National Education Association, 1958).

[5] Katherine E. D'Evelyn, *Individual Parent-Teacher Conferences: A Manual for Teachers of Young Children* (New York: Bureau of Publications, Teachers College, Columbia University, 1959).

[6] Ruth Strang, *Reporting to Parents* (New York: Bureau of Publications, Teachers College, Columbia University, 1958).

[7] American Council of Education, *op. cit.*

[8] Driscoll, *op. cit.,* p. 24.

child has to learn in a step-by-step procedure what most other children learn casually. The importance of positive reinforcement, the use of punishment, the negative effects of failure, the rules for maximum use of transfer in learning, the role of emotions and self-concept, and the place of motivation and practice are all lessons in basic psychology important to parents.

How many times has a parent faced personal failure in his own estimation because, as he expresses it, "I keep telling her, and she just doesn't seem to learn." Parents don't always know that "just telling" is not enough if they are really to teach some children. Helping parents see the human side, the humorous side, and the way their child sees the problem may make a difference in the human relationships of a family. A constant effort of the school should be to keep the parent informed in the broadest terms of what the child has done, is doing, and is capable of doing. The information, of course, should be expressed sympathetically, realistically, and professionally.

Community Resources, Work Opportunities, Delinquency

Brief, though vital, consideration must be given to the place of the broader community in the education of the slow learner. Although the primary responsibility for health, education, and all other major factors related to the development of children are retained by the family and home, society has accepted the responsibility for supplementing that key source. It pays the educational bills, designates who shall teach, and decides how long the educational process will continue.

Slow learners do not, of course, all come from poor neighborhoods, but enough of them do for special attention to be paid to neighborhood poverty, overcrowdedness, and lack of education and play facilities as contributing factors to the incidence of lagging school accomplishment. Responsibilities accrue to the community, either narrowly or broadly defined, to recognize its deficiencies and explore ways of solving them, to know what its schools are like (in comparison with others), and to realize how much it may be contributing to the slow learning of those who are not inherently slower mentally and to the depressed learning of those who are inherently slower. The large amount of unequal opportunity which exists for children, both in the community and in the schools in these communities, is vividly pictured in Conant's description of the child of the city slum in contrast to the child of the middle and upper class suburban environment.[9]

Hull and Cummings describe the picture Conant presents as being very much the same and perhaps even worse today than the condition of youth reported in 1937 after a survey by the American Youth Commission of the American Council on Education. Their information about the problems of youth in the middle 1930's declared that at least 40 per cent of the young people between 16 and 24 years of age were out of school and unemployed. Many had appalling health problems, including venereal disease. Many could barely read or write; many were delinquent; and many of the girls had illegitimate children. Since that time we have had the Civilian Conservation Corps and the National Youth Authority attempting to provide for employment with public funds, until World War II made those programs unnecessary. Today the drop-out figures and unemployed numbers are again dangerously large in number. We again have Commissions appointed by the President for the purpose of studying problems of youth employment and delinquency. The public again talks about programs such as the CCC and NYA.

> Cultural incompatibility and educational inadequacy are not new phenomena, nor are they more repugnant to American morality today than in the past. But mobility has brought the problem to the fore and has made its solution more urgent. Current efforts to help the disadvantaged American are inadequate. The society must find ways to help him overcome his handicaps and find the opportunities which the American tradition promises him.[10]

Conant reminds us that emphasis has been placed on the need to improve programs for the bright student, but we must also remember that half the population has below-average ability. He suggests a broad program in education, rather than one in which students

---

[9] Conant, *op. cit.*
[10] J. Dan Hull and Howard H. Cummings, "How Fare American Youth in 1962?" *School Life*, Vol. 44, No. 4 (January-February, 1962), pp. 13–16.

fill their programs with electives in music, crafts, and auto mechanics.[11]

In *Education and the Disadvantaged American,* the authors state, "If present trends are not reversed, half the inhabitants of the large city of 1970 may be disadvantaged—persons unable to participate constructively in their society." [12] The school needs to coordinate its work with the community agencies and these agencies need to coordinate their services. The typical fragmentation of services to families in need leads to treatment of symptoms and disposal of cases, without any attempt to provide leadership which is aimed at the basic problems. School social workers who can integrate and understand the school's role and the role of integrated community effort can be key personnel. The necessity for integrated efforts between the school, community agencies, labor unions, industry, government, and business to integrate efforts and plan for long-range programs to solve the basic problems caused by unequal opportunities to the culturally deprived, the disadvantaged, and the second-class citizen is basic to any real attempt any one group may make.

What goes on in the school cannot be divorced from the community. A teacher was quoted in New York City as saying, "We do quite well with these children in the lower grades. Each of us is for the few hours of the school day an acceptable substitute for the mother. But when they reach 10, 11, or 12 years of age we lose them. At that time the street takes over. In terms of schoolwork, progress ceases; indeed many pupils begin to go backward in their studies!" [13]

President Kennedy received from his special panel studying the problems of mental retardation a far-reaching program with recommendations for extensive community action to combat what the President termed as the nation's most important and neglected health problem. Among the major recommendations by the panel were:

1. An increase in basic and applied research, including eventual establishment of 10 key research centers.

---

11 Conant, *op. cit.,* pp. 105–9.
12 Educational Policies Commission, *Education and the Disadvantaged American* (Washington, D.C.: National Education Association 1962), p. 10.
13 Conant, *op. cit.,* p. 21.

2. The establishment of a national research of learning.

3. The creation of a new pattern of institutional care of the retarded, including small residential treatment centers instead of large institutions that now house up to 5,000 or more patients.

4. The expansion of Federal maternal and child health grant programs to aid the "high risk" pregnancy cases in the low-income groups.

5. The recruitment and training of an additional 55,000 teachers for the mentally retarded. There now are only about 20,000 such special teachers in this nation.[14]

Adequate diagnostic facilities must be considered one of the foundation stones in building a sound community program for all children who indicate some special needs. Only severe problems are usually identified early in the child's life. For the average child, a problem is not recognized until failure in school becomes a pattern or matter of concern. A few parents may be sufficiently sophisticated and knowledgeable about what to expect of child behavior that they seek specific answers to questions related to the child's strengths and weaknesses. Diagnostic data need to determine the nature and degree of any special problem and must help the parents to understand and plan according to the best information available. Considerable evidence exists as to the value of early identification and diagnosis of problem areas. Sometimes medical intervention can make the difference between solving the problem or the existence of something with which the child will have to live.

Early identification is stressed as a preventive measure which runs as a thread through most of the literature pertaining to the problems of delinquency. Kvaraceus states: "To sum up the research of the last six years: In spite of the mythology and folklore that persists in approaches to delinquency in most communities, there are now discernible a number of promising practices aimed to prevent and control norm-violating behavior—practices which appear to be relevant to the factors which germinate and cause such behavior." [15]

Leadership must frequently come from the school in letting the

[14] Marjorie Hunter, "Plan for Retarded Given to President," *The New York Times,* Western Edition (October 16, 1962).

[15] William C. Kvaraceus, "The Delinquent," *Review of Educational Research,* Vol. XXIX, No. 5 (December, 1959), p. 550.

community know about these problems. Educators have sometimes been remiss in their duty to a public that supports them by not speaking loudly enough about their inability to solve the problems assigned to them. Information regarding drop-outs and differences in intellectual ability are among the subjects demanding the best in school public relations approaches.

Role of the Federal Government

The 1960 White House Conference on Children and Youth brought more than 7500 people together for 5 days to consider the various ways in which youth might be helped to "reach their full potential for a creative life in freedom and dignity." [16] Fifty states, the District of Columbia, Puerto Rico, the Virgin Islands, Guam, and American Samoa participated. Twelve states specify that young people must be included in their follow-up organizational structures. Forty-three states have committees which include young people as active participants in some phase of their programs. Problems of unemployed youth, juvenile delinquency, and family life education programs are among areas of study with programs of action evolved. The problems of school drop-outs, youth employment, and school work programs are the center of attention in numerous states today.

The program of improved guidance services has been given assistance from the National Defense Education Act of 1958. Conant adds the following to the problems of guidance services: "To my mind, guidance officers, especially in the large cities, ought to be given the responsibility for following the post-high school careers of youth from the time they leave school until they are 21 years of age." [17]

While the protection of children from illegal and harmful employment continues to be a need, particularly for families related to migratory agricultural work, another problem faces most communities. It is the need for increased job opportunities and on-the-job training programs in the community for young people, a need rec-

[16] Frances Schmidt and Mildred I. French, "White House Conference Follow-up Within the States," *Children*, Vol. 9, No. 1 (January-February, 1962), pp. 3–8.
[17] James B. Conant, "Social Dynamite in Our Large Cities," *Children*, Vol. 8, No. 5 (September-October, 1961), p. 168.

ognized by secondary education personnel and supported in the studies of the White House Conference.

Cohen and Kapp suggest the following specific proposals as community solutions to the youth-employment problem:

1. Develop job opportunities for inexperienced youth. They suggest the use of a federal program to subsidize work and training projects similar to those of the Civilian Conservation Corps of the thirties.

2. Improve and expand vocational guidance and counseling services.

3. Increase and improve vocational training and work-education programs with emphasis on reaching young people who are considered potential drop-outs. Reference is made to the success of labor, industry, and community leadership working with the personnel of the Great Cities School Improvement Program. The St. Louis Board of Education has organized a work-study program for potential drop-outs.

4. Increase on-the-job training and apprenticeship programs for all youth.

5. Arouse labor and management to take action against racial discrimination in hiring, upgrading, and firing.

6. Increase efforts to raise vocational sights of youngsters from low economic areas. Again the Higher Horizons Program is cited as one approach. The National Urban League is cited for its sponsorship of career clubs in 20 cities as part of its talent identification program.

7. Provide special help for school drop-outs.

8. Give expert help to rural youth coming into cities to find jobs.

9. Study future manpower needs.

10. Work for faster economic growth.[18]

Communities can react only when they are informed, when the facts of educational loss are presented to them, and when they realize how they may be failing in their responsibility for local solution of major problems. The community's efforts to help the parent of the slow learner can ultimately pay rich dividends for both.

---

[18] Eli E. Cohen and Louise Kapp, "Youth and Work: The Second Challenge," *Children*, Vol. 9, No. 2 (March-April, 1962), 82–83.

CHAPTER IV

The School

Although some of the problems of slow learners reach a climax in intensity within the home, a whole series of long-range climaxes emerge after school entry. For the first time, strangers become directly involved in learning and adjustment problems. Thousands of schools and teachers daily exert intensive efforts to ease these difficulties, many of which have been accumulating since birth.

Organization and Administrative Structure

In many school districts administrative provisions related to promotion, grading, special classes, partial separation, grouping, teacher aptitudes, and the use of ungraded or unlabeled class levels are under almost constant discussion and evaluation. Inevitably involved is the cost factor related to these matters. Concern is also expressed through conferences, reports, and more informal approaches to a long list of additional school adaptations to meet the needs of the slow learner. These adaptations include the following:

1. Provide suitable reading, reference, programmed learning, audio-visual, and other commercial and teacher-made materials.
2. Set up teacher in-service preparation related to child study techniques and to adapted methods for teaching slow learners.
3. Organize a cumulative record system to which all teaching, guidance, and administrative personnel contribute, and which all use profitably to help advance the education of slow children.
4. Provide for teacher-counselor conferences, teacher visitation to other teachers and schools where programs are adapted with some success to meet individual needs, and articulation between the elementary and secondary levels so educational continuity is eased for slow learners.
5. Set a curriculum framework that provides for flexibility in organizing appropriate blocks of work for individual and small groups of children.

6. Consider the special needs of schools in rural areas, in poor
neighborhoods, and in overcrowded districts.

The literature on slow children represents many conflicts in relation to programs existing for the slow learner. G. Orville Johnson
discusses the large amount of emphasis which has been placed on
individual differences, but which has resulted in no real program
geared to the special group of needs which identify the slow learner.[1]

On the other hand, the Jewett and Hull study reports that in the
sample of 1200 secondary schools to which their questionnaire was
sent, 795 usable returns reported that schools are making more administrative provisions for slow learners than they are making for
rapid learners. In general, senior high schools are making the greatest number of adaptations, and junior high schools the fewest. There
was revealed in most of the 23 provisions listed on the questionnaire a direct relationship between the size of schools and the number of administrative provisions for rapid and slow learners.
Comparatively fewer schools, according to the survey, are using
homogeneous grouping today than 20 years ago. About half the
schools in this study, however, reported such grouping.[2]

Efforts are frequently made to cut class size in order to increase
individualized teaching, although research is inconclusive on the
relationship between class size and effective instruction. The N.E.A.
Research Division made a study of teachers' and principals' experience relative to class size and stated: "Although research on the
best size of class for effective teaching may be inconclusive, the
majority of both elementary school teachers and principals agree
that a class of 20-24 pupils is the best size."[3] McLoughlin[4] and
McKenna[5] both reported advantages in having small classes, since
individual differences could more adequately be understood. Early
studies on this subject were interested mainly in the achievement
and promotion factors relative to class size. Achievement skills

[1] G. Orville Johnson, *Education For the Slow Learners* (Englewood Cliffs, N.J.:
Prentice-Hall, Inc., 1963), pp. 12–17.

[2] Jewett and Hull, *op. cit.,* p. 13.

[3] NEA Research Division, "Best Class Size," *NEA Research Bulletin,* Vol. 39,
No. 4 (December, 1961), p. 107.

[4] W. P. McLoughlin, "Class Size Affects Learning Ability," *School Executive,*
Vol. 75 (March, 1956), pp. 91–93.

[5] Bernard H. McKenna, "Greater Learning in Smaller Classes," *NEA Journal*
(October, 1957), pp. 437–38.

as measured by standardized tests are not affected by the factor of class size. In measuring other than scholastic achievement, however, B. H. McKenna cites guidelines with the understanding that no one rule exists and that no absolute decision can be made upon the appropriate range of class sizes, either in elementary schools or in high schools without considering certain very crucial related policies:

1. Educational purpose must be taken into account.
2. Quality of staff should not be sacrificed for small class size.
3. The characteristics of pupils is a key factor in class-size decisions.
4. The many other important factors which go to make up teacher load have to be taken into consideration.
5. The effect on teacher morale has to be thoughtfully considered.
6. A balance should be maintained between classroom teachers and other specialists.
7. Teaching load should be equalized.
8. Class size and teaching load should be reviewed periodically.
9. The staff should be prepared for any anticipated change (either smaller or larger) in class size.
10. Community understanding, participation, and acceptance are prerequisites for any consistent and genuine policy on class size.[6]

A key factor in the school's approach to its slow learners is based on the attitudes, understandings, and knowledge of its staff. Do its members know how many slow learners they have? Are they aware of the causes and characteristics of slow learners? Do they recognize and fully accept their responsibilities related to identification, instruction, and evaluation of children and programs? Have they established close and cooperative relationships with parents? Have they made, and are they continuing to make, efforts toward accomplishing the objectives listed above, and others related to them? Do they realize that academic learning is only part of a child's life, and may be an especially limited segment for some of these children? Do they know how they contribute to (and how they might avoid) intellectual snobbery among children, which sometimes evolves from concentration on unrealistic academic achievement, report cards, and retention in the grades?

[6] Bernard H. McKenna, "What About Class Size?" *New York State Education,* Vol. XLV, No. 2 (November, 1957), pp. 100–101.

Schools are usually aware of their problems, of the insecure and the isolates, of the ways in which self-respect is limited or destroyed, and of unfair competition between unequals. Their efforts are becoming more intensified every year toward solving them.

Current Practices

Schools generally attempt to adapt their educational programs to the needs of slow learners (as well as to all other groups) within their limitations of qualified personnel, awareness of the problems, and money available. They have been helped by the alertness of textbook publishers, pressure of parents, and the needs of a country more aware than ever that each individual must be educated to his capacity in order to make a maximum contribution for the common good.

Elementary schools. In low income areas where the largest number of slow-learning children live, the schools in general have a larger proportion of older, more inadequate physical buildings; fewer cafeteria, library, and recreational facilities; a larger percentage of unqualified or less competent teachers; larger classes and more overcrowding in general; less parent participation; poorer attendance rates; more sickness; more transient enrollments; a smaller number of remedial and social welfare services available; more delinquency; more nonreaders; and more school failures. The customary practice of grouping first grade children on the basis of reading readiness achievement scores becomes for many children of lesser opportunity a channel through which they move in repeated failure so far as the school is concerned.[7]

Many practices to help slow learners have been developed, based on their appropriateness for particular schools, communities, and children. Thoughtful administrators and teachers study those in operation elsewhere, but are careful in their borrowing and adaptations. Samples of practices most frequently discussed in the literature on this subject are listed below. The list is neither all-inclusive nor arranged in order of frequency:

---

[7] Sexton, *op. cit.*

1. Grouping on basis of achievement, using flexibility; not same group for all subjects and activities.

2. Strengthened, and sometimes lengthened, readiness programs.

3. Promotion with chronological age groups, based to a large extent on extensive research related to retention and its ineffectiveness toward increasing academic achievement.

4. Simplification of materials, techniques, and experiences for slow-learning children; adaptive measures related to drill, review, and concrete usage rather than abstract rules; use of high interest-low ability reading materials; use of programmed learning materials, especially appropriate because of the success factor, small steps, and sequential organization.

5. Efforts to cover different subject matter and in a different way, rather than exactly the same areas more slowly.

6. Program adaptations in both teaching and guidance, based on junior or senior high school as terminal education.

7. Use of home rooms or self-contained classrooms for increased stability and continuity.

8. Participation in school activities. "If a school newspaper is thought to be good for the bright pupils, it is doubly good for the slow-learning ones—not so good for the newspaper, perhaps, but good for the pupils." [8]

9. Expansion of guidance and counseling facilities and activities.

10. Inclusion of the child in the planning, through such practices as teacher-pupil conferences or daily "contractual" arrangements.

The Great Cities School Improvement Program now operates in 13 large cities under the general guidance of the Ford Foundation. The goals are placed on programs aimed at meeting more adequately the needs and backgrounds of children in depressed areas. In Detroit two elementary schools and one junior high school served as pilot schools to demonstrate some of the benefits already accrued in reports from the experimental programs.[9] An ungraded primary unit was inaugurated after considerable study in one of the elementary schools. The children were organized into groups, according to reading achievement and reading skills. These groups allowed a child to progress from one level to the next according to his ability and achievement, thus permitting the slow child to take more time to master skills. The average time to finish this primary cycle was

---

[8] Featherstone, *op. cit.*, p. 34.
[9] Report, Board of Education, Detroit, "Great Cities Program for School Improvement in Areas Where Pupils Have Limited Backgrounds," October 22, 1960.

2½ years, with some children finishing earlier and others taking 3 or 4 years.

In each of the schools, special materials served to bridge the gap between school and home vocabularies. Extensive use of experience stories, teacher-made materials, and experiments with new reading materials became part of the program. Individual needs of children were considered by recognizing birthdays, increased emphasis on dramatization, and an over-all emphasis on ways to increase a child's sense of identity and recognition. The same teacher kept her group of pupils longer than the regular school year, and this was believed to have certain beneficial results. Use of team teaching, the increased use of audio-visual materials, and an additional clerk-typist in each building to help produce teacher-made materials were components of the total program.

At the junior high school level the program was planned under six department heads who made an effort to enrich and adapt instruction so that it would become more meaningful and purposeful to individual students. Emphasis was placed on identifying students with particular learning problems and providing needed help. Field trips, involvement of the children, the use of special personnel, a school-community coordinator, the services of a social worker as a visiting teacher, a coaching teacher who offered a remedial program with a mental health approach, the involvement of the community agencies and their personnel, and extensive contacts with parents were all used.

A cooperative nursery school was also introduced. It brought three- and four-year-olds into the program to give a more adequate apperceptive background which could lead to more success in school work.

A New England survey in 1956 summarized information on slow learner programs and related matters. Only six schools of 45 replying stated they had any organized program for slow learners in grades seven, eight, and nine. Nineteen definitely stated they had none. Twelve school systems evidently had programs for mentally retarded pupils, who were classified as slow learners. The conclusions based on the study of the reports received were stated as follows:

1. There was no general agreement on a definition of the "slow learner."

2. There was evidence that mentally retarded children and slow learners were in the same classification in many school systems.

3. There are many school systems which do not provide definite measures to meet the needs of the slow learner.

4. Many schools recognize the problem but do not know how to cope with it. Quote: "When you do find the answer to the 'slow learner,' for heaven's sake let us know."

5. Many things are being done in an attempt to meet the problem of the slow learner, when the school systems as a whole are studied. However, very few, if any, individual schools reported definite co-ordinated measures being provided.

6. There was little evidence submitted concerning the effectiveness of the measures taken by schools to meet the problem.

7. The questionnaire used, because of its generality, was not clear to those reporting, principally because no definition of the "slow learner" was formulated.

8. There was a dependence upon low I.Q. scores for identifying a slow learner, and little was mentioned about boys and girls with normal I.Q.'s who are slow learners or poor "achievers" for many reasons other than low I.Q. scores.

9. If the sampling of this survey is typical, it indicates that the problem of providing for the slow learner is widespread and is generally recognized, but needs further definition and attention, with more definite organization of procedures of instruction as an integral part of the junior high school program.[10]

Secondary Schools. If it is true that ". . . pupils with I.Q.'s below 90 are practically certain to fail in such subjects as algebra and Latin and are not likely to graduate from high school . . . and that 75 per cent of those who test below average mentally will fail in more than one-half of their studies during their first year in high school," [11] then the special consideration being given to slow learners on the high school level in recent years is worthy of attention. Children forced to attend school by home and social pressures warrant programs that are within their intellectual grasp. The resultant adjustments in many communities are toward prevocational and technical high schools, and in others toward a modification of aca-

---

[10] New England School Development Council, *Some Basic Educational Principles and Their Applications in Early Adolescence* (Cambridge: Spaulding House, 1956), p. 45.

[11] Lillian G. Portenier, *Pupils of Low Mentality in High School* (New York: Bureau of Publications, Teachers College, Columbia University, 1933), p. 1.

demic content and standards. "To place a dull-normal child in a school with a curriculum designed for the small group who plan to go to college is like throwing a non-swimmer into the ocean." [12]

When queried on the subject, high school principals have generally felt that adaptations should be along these lines: not as much class work and not as difficult work; individual coaching or remedial work in special subjects; and a special curriculum, including some academic work, but with emphasis on the practical and vocational. High schools themselves were found to make more provisions for slow learners than for rapid learners, to be aware of individual differences and making efforts to provide for them, and to make less use of homogeneous grouping than they did 20 years ago.[13]

Jewett and Hull summarize results concerning instructional provisions and procedures used by teachers considered extremely effective in teaching rapid learners and slow learners. Their questionnaire was addressed to the heads of departments in English, social studies, mathematics, science, home economics, and industrial arts.[14]

Tucker, working in an upper economic class community, states that a slow learner is surrounded by certain pressures which result in frustrations created by his inability to do the work regular students do. He believes that separation has created more problems and has been responsible for feelings resulting from membership in the "dumb class," which led to becoming a drop-out. He states that the program for a slow learner includes:

1. Individual approach by a study of his personal and educational history.
2. A study of his weaknesses and strengths.
3. Cooperation and understanding of his parents and educational history.
4. Courses adjusted to his individual needs.
5. Participation in regular classes, providing association with the regular students is a learning experience.
6. Due recognition of his accomplishments in some written form

[12] Kirk, *Teaching Reading to Slow-Learning Children*, pp. 175–76.
[13] Kenneth N. Nickel, "Better Education for Nonacademic Pupils," *North Central Association Quarterly*, Vol. XXXI, No. 4 (April, 1957).
[14] Jewett and Hull, *op. cit.*

comparable to that of all students at the conclusion of his school work.[15]

New York began a program in 1956 aimed at the underprivileged child who was not succeeding in school. The program featured group and individual guidance and counseling for the children and their parents, clinical services, intensive courses in English, and other extras, including trips to cultural and artistic events. It was the success of this program which led to other similar programs under the Higher Horizons Project in New York City, and finally spread to the Great Cities School Improvement Program, including Baltimore, Buffalo, Boston, Chicago, Cleveland, Detroit, Los Angeles, Milwaukee, Philadelphia, Pittsburgh, San Francisco, St. Louis, and Washington, D.C. Final summaries and evaluations have yet to be written for all of these experimental programs. Enough has been written and sufficient studies have already been released, however, to indicate that many new and rewarding techniques, methods, practices, and materials are already in evidence.

Secondary schools have for the past 50 years offered school work programs. The most common have been identified as cooperative education, occupational experience, diversified occupations, school-work, work-study, work-education, job-experience, education for work, work experience, and many others. Increased automation and technology place a challenging task before those who train youth. Vocational curriculum should be broadly based; it should not become the traditional haven for students who have not been able to succeed in other programs. The high school cooperative program introduces the student to the distributive education field. On-the-job training in distributive occupations is combined with classroom instruction, and a distributive education club program is regarded as a supplement to classroom instruction. Community businessmen are often the key to the success of this program.[16]

A nonprofit corporation Careers for Youth is privately administered and financed, but works in cooperation with the Phoenix,

[15] Ruel E. Tucker, "A Program for Slow Learners," *Bulletin of the National Association of Secondary-School Principals,* Vol. 36, No. 185 (March, 1952), pp. 333–36.
[16] U.S. Department of Health, Education, and Welfare, *Distributive Education, A Study of Curriculum Development in the High School Cooperative Program* (Washington, D.C.: U.S. Office of Education, 1960).

Arizona, schools. It began as a pilot group for selected seventh and eighth graders and added ninth graders the following year. Its purpose is to provide an answer to the drop-out rates among deprived groups by providing scholarships for children who would otherwise be forced to leave school before graduation. Ninety-two per cent of the Negro students and eighty-five per cent of the Spanish-speaking students in the Phoenix area do not finish high school. Textbooks and costs total approximately 62 dollars a year in high school, and many get discouraged. The program organizes students into Career Clubs which meet regularly with qualified people to discuss job qualifications, preparation, job content, and rewards.[17]

An increasing amount of concern has been demonstrated in recent years on the secondary level toward the slow learner. Until the past few years, many secondary administrators and teachers felt that this educational problem belonged (and should stay) in the

	269 public high schools	328 Catholic high schools
Teacher marks	1	1
Group intelligence tests	2	2
Teachers' estimates of school achievement	3	3
Information on vocational plans	4	5.5
Information on physical health	5	11
Guidance counselor's appraisal of pupils' interests, abilities, aptitudes	6	12.5
Standardized achievement tests	7	5.5
Information on reading habits and reading interests	8	7.5
Information on home environment	9	7.5
Anecdotal reports and records	10	17.5
Information on personality adjustment	11	9
Teachers' estimates of pupils' aptitudes	13	4
Teachers' estimates of intelligence	13	12.5
Information on social adjustment	15.5	14
Information on physical maturity	15.5	17.5
Standardized aptitude tests in specific fields	17	16
Individualized intelligence tests	18	19
Homeroom advisor's estimate of pupils' interests, abilities, aptitudes	19	10
Parental appraisal of pupils' interests, abilities, aptitudes	20	15
Appraisal of school psychologist	Not available	20

[17] Maggie Savoy, "Careers for Youth Finds a Way," *The Arizona Republic* (April 8, 1962).

elementary school. The elementary schools which attempted to cope with it found, however, that sheer age and size interfered—factors which forced the concern to move on.

The techniques used in public and Catholic high schools for the identification of slow learners are indicated on page 60 in rank order, based on extent of use.[18]

In the chart that follows, the items indicate a strong awareness of educational problems of slow learners and the numerous efforts being made to help solve them in many high schools: [19]

	Per cent of 263 public high schools	Per cent of 328 Catholic high schools
Teachers furnished guidance information pertinent to students	85	92
Teachers assigned on basis of traits and interests suitable for work	81	73
Regular classes furnished with additional study materials and learning aids	77	79
Job placement service	76	49
Easy study materials related to students' interests	74	67
Space, furniture, and equipment for flexible grouping	68	47
Low ability classes in certain subjects	57	75
Supervised work experiences after school hours	53	28
Ability (homogeneous) classes on basis of I.Q., reading ability, previous grades, social maturity	49	60
Remedial sections where performance is below capacity in basic skills	46	58
Teachers assigned on basis of training and experience with slow learners	45	45
Individualized instruction outside of regular class hours	43	67
Flexible graduation requirement as to credit	40	35
Promotion of students on basis of effort	39	66
Transfer to special school encouraged	38	58
Summer sessions provided	36	40
Regularly scheduled guidance program for the direction of low ability students	Not available	36
Promotion of students on basis of physical and social development	Not available	20

[18] Thomas J. Frain, *Administrative and Instructional Provisions for Rapid and Slow Learners in Catholic Secondary Schools* (Washington, D.C.: The Catholic University of America Press, 1956), pp. 36–37.

[19] *Ibid.*, pp. 22–23.

Promotion and Grading Policies

"One of the great tragedies of education is that too often the statement, 'We are concerned with the individual,' means that we are concerned because the individual does not measure up to the standards arbitrarily set for him."[20] As indicated earlier, however, a trend seems to be apparent to promote children with their chronological age group. The relative ineffectiveness of retention in contributing to increased academic achievement, as shown by much of the research on this subject, is probably the reason behind the trend. Nonpromotion as either a threat or a practice has contributed little, if at all, to academic gain generally, although in some individual cases it may be the correct solution for a problem.

Whenever possible, schools seem to use the aim that is simple to express, but difficult to implement: the best setting, the best group, and the best teacher for each child. Although regrouping is necessary from time to time, reasonable stability and permanence are important ingredients in the progress of slow learners.

Despite specific subject-matter handicaps, the current tendency is to move fourteen-year-olds on to high school because of the age and size factors. Whether or not that is done in a particular community may depend on whether or not the high school has adapted its program to meet needs of slow learners. Absence of such adaptations on the high school level and provisions for them in the elementary school may, from a practical point of view, make retention a better solution.

Some schools solve the promotion problem by seeking answers to one or more of these questions: Does he accomplish one year's growth in a year on the basis of achievement testing? What will help this particular child more, promotion or retention? Are our standards applicable to him? All of the controversial factors related to social promotion are part of this subject. The most sound approach seems to be to view it from the child's position, and seek a solution that will contribute most to his well-being now and in the future.

Another controversial area is in the realm of grading. Should the

---

[20] "A Tragedy of Education," *Personnel and Guidance Journal* (November, 1955), p. 153.

child be graded on the basis of his own ability, receiving a top grade if he is working to his capacity, or should firm standards be maintained for grading purposes? Some schools support one of those two viewpoints without qualification. Others use more flexible approaches based on transcript and cumulative folder information, which reflect the child and his specific accomplishments and limitations in a more personalized manner.

Special Classes

Relatively few schools and school districts attempt to educate slow learners in special classes. Where such classes have been set up, it is sometimes found that they become a repository for misfits, a place where the delinquent, the emotionally disturbed, and the unduly shy are sent along with the slow learner. In most cases where solutions of this kind are attempted, they seldom remain in operation long.

Some of the reasons offered by those who support special classes are of the following type: (1) better possibility of achieving and of being accepted and respected by classmates; (2) easier to adapt the educational program to them; (3) reduces costs due to pupil failure. The reasons for not having special classes are along this line: (1) children would be stigmatized; (2) such classes are undemocratic; (3) they are too costly; (4) they deprive the slower children of a chance to adapt to the kind of society in which they will be living; (5) they may become a catch-all for problems; and (6) they may exaggerate differences.

G. Orville Johnson believes that children should be grouped because of the similarity of both their characteristics and educational needs. The child whose learning rates are at a slower pace than those of children in the usual classroom requires a set of goals and techniques different from those of the child who is emotionally maladjusted or who, for various reasons, needs a remedial program. Johnson would also integrate these children with the regular classes in any one activity in which the child can perform on a relatively equal basis. This would require an individual rather than a group process. He also believes children should be housed in neighborhood schools so that they are given every opportunity to feel that they belong and are like the other children. This is in contrast to the practice in many places where children are transported to a school for various reasons. A second aspect of the neighborhood school is the use of neighborhood resources in curriculum development.[21]

In smaller schools the question may be answered easily, since there may be too few students available for the special classes. Both small and large schools might be reluctant about setting up special classes because of their own philosophy against them, parental objections, or official regulations. Most schools that have considered them at all generally veto the idea because they feel that segregation is a solution only in situations where an integrated approach cannot be used, as for more severely retarded children. Too many schools have coped successfully with the slow learner in regular classrooms for any large number of others to view separation as the best administrative answer. Whether or not special classes are set up, the important issues still remain in the areas of curricular adjustments, appropriate teacher assignments, adapted materials, and student security and accomplishment.

Curriculum

A one-sided approach to curriculum from the point of view of content is too limiting for any child. Concentration on reading, science, mathematics, art, music, or vocational subjects to the almost complete exclusion of other areas would not prepare a person to cope with the complexities of modern life. The ability to communicate with others, appreciation for the democratic way of life, an understanding of the world, and preparation for making a living are all necessary toward creating the well-rounded person. A curriculum based on breadth, with depth appropriately adjusted, is the goal for schools attempting to educate slow learners well. One source views this objective in the following way: [22]

1. Developmental approach—based on experiences for effective living and for future needs, on the realization that the length of education may be limited and that some areas should be considered

---

[21] G. Orville Johnson, *The Slow Learner—A Second-Class Citizen?*, pp. 34–36.
[22] Bloom and Murray, *op. cit.*

earlier (consumer education, for example) on the belief that complex subjects of questionable value be omitted.

2. Modification approach—based on a change in amount of content.

3. Simplification approach—based on an adjustment downward in levels of difficulty.

4. Basic essentials approach—based on the inclusion of minimum essentials at an understandable level.

5. Individualized approach—based on an adaptation to purpose, personality, capacity, and rate of learning.

Organizational plans absorbing the preceding five approaches may be set up in a variety of ways. The child may be with the same teacher all the time, for part of the day in a core program (bringing together areas like English, social studies, and mathematics), or for only one subject. Most plans are based on the belief that slow learners should be with other children in classroom settings for at least part of each day.

Although the potentialities of each child must be considered in adjusting a curriculum to him, generalized kinds of predictions have been made. One source states that ". . . from knowledge of a pupil's general intelligence we can make very reliable predictions as to his capacity for reading and for arithmetic, somewhat less reliable predictions as to his aptitude for spelling or mechanics, and that our predictions concerning his ability to draw, sing, or play musical instruments should be given without confidence in their reliability, if given at all." [23]

In the area of reading it has often been stated that there are no special methods necessary for teaching slow learners. Even more than for other children, however, an orderly and systematic approach is necessary, with special attention to (1) reading readiness, (2) building vocabulary and methods of word recognition, (3) setting up individual standards of expectancy, and (4) selection of reading materials. Meaningful use of phonics, experience charts, auditory and visual activities and games, mechanical aids, basic reading series (plus the teacher's manuals), supplementary reading materials, and workbooks (not used as busywork) are all important

---

[23] Leta Hollingworth, *Special Talents and Effects* (New York: The Macmillan Company, 1923), p. 37.

parts of the program. The teaching of reading to slow learners may begin later and last longer than it would for other children.

When slow learners are capable of reading the primers, these beginning books may have lost their attraction for them. A similar problem follows through the grades as ability levels lag behind interests. A broad area of literature for children has developed in recent years to meet that need. A few samples of these high interest-low ability (vocabulary) materials are listed below:

American Adventure Series. Wheeler Publishing Company, 2831 South Parkway, Chicago 16, Illinois.

American Heritage Series. American Book Company, 501 Elm Street, Dallas 2, Texas.

Childhood of Famous Americans Series. Bobbs-Merrill Company, Inc., 730 N. Meridian Street, Indianapolis 7, Indiana.

Classmate Editions. Lyons and Carnahan, 376 South Pasadena Avenue, Pasadena 2, California.

Cowboy Sam Series. Beckley-Cardy, 1900 N. Narragansett, Chicago 39, Illinois.

First Books Series. Franklin Watts, 699 Madison Avenue, New York 21, New York.

Landmark Books, Allabout Books. Random House, 457 Madison Avenue, New York 22, New York.

Skill Builders. Reader's Digest Educational Service, 353 Fourth Avenue, New York 10, New York.

True Book Series. Children's Press, Jackson and Racine, Chicago 7, Illinois.

Although students limited in reading speed and comprehension are frequently slow learners, this is not a necessary relationship. Because reading problems stem from a variety of sources, one cannot assume that an intellectual handicap is the sole cause. A student behind in reading skills is not always a laggard in other subject areas, although there is often a close relationship; improved reading ability frequently brings with it a lower number of failures in other school subjects.

For slow learners as well as others, reading should be approached from various directions, for enjoyment as well as information. Discovering causes, eliminating difficulties, and providing materials from the great choice available will help answer statements such as the following one: "The schools are failing to provide an educational system which will encourage the dull-normal child to learn to read so that he will read to learn." [24]

The New York City Board of Education has said that it will use only books which deal adequately with minorities. Detroit has introduced three new primers whose characters are mostly Negro children. In the low-normal classes of the Speyer School in New York City, reading was not made a primary or exclusive tool of learning in a curriculum set up on conventional subject-matter lines. Instead, an activity type of program was used where more use was made of projects, construction activities, discussion, and visitation. Reading was integrated into the full program, rather than singled out for special and continuous attention. Conclusions drawn were that the Speyer students acquired as much reading ability, read more widely, and enjoyed reading more than did the students from more conventional settings with whom they were compared. Most writers in the field, however, cling to the importance of the more systematic, orderly approach to teaching reading to slow learners.

Teaching in the other language arts areas also has to be adapted to the maturation or readiness factor. The ability to talk, understand, write, and listen are usually delayed in slow learning children. By not isolating the development of language skills from the rest of the curriculum and by using group discussions, choral speaking, recordings, carefully selected stories and books, and informal conversations, the language arts areas become of value to these children. If they write what they need when the need arises, and if their dramatization, sociodramas, discussions of activities, and oral expression are based on what they care about, the simple language and vocabulary skills of value to them will probably evolve.

The necessity of realistic objectives is apparent when one observes the inarticulate writing and speech and poor spelling and punctuation which may be the result of drudgery and meaningless drill. Writing and speaking with purpose after making detailed preparation can result in fluency of a basic nature.

As in reading, the area of arithmetic does not demand special methods for slow learners, but it does call for adaptations in the ones most commonly used. Advice from experts in the field is usu-

---

[24] Kirk, *Teaching Reading to Slow-Learning Children,* p. 178.

ally based on these suggestions: Make it real and concrete by using current experiences; base arithmetic learnings on a systematic approach; don't go too fast, and don't assume concepts are learned "once and for all"; use special aids—flash cards, number games, flannel boards, or devices based on number and size; consider carefully individual readiness for new ideas and concepts; use practice materials, but not for themselves alone and not based merely on repetition without another more important purpose; use a good textbook series; use an oral approach if reading abilities interfere; try for accuracy more than speed.

Just as in other areas, it is important for the teacher himself to have a sound background in and an affirmative attitude toward the subject.

A certain group of mathematics teachers met regularly from 6:30 A.M. to 8 A.M. on the teachers' own time in an effort to find ways to put new meaning into teaching mathematics to high school students who could not find reasons for studying math. Patterned after an outline suggested by the National Science Foundation, their experiment appears to have generated positive results. It is perhaps indicative of a new emphasis which Stratemeyer refers to as curriculum from the standpoint of persistent life situations which the child must meet.

It is the field of science that the recommendations toward concreteness of teaching and the use of materials that can be handled and manipulated take on most meaning. Simple experiments, collecting, field trips, and a classroom science corner can all be adapted to slow learners' levels of ability and interest. Various areas of science can be used as motivation toward other subject fields, to establish rapport with teachers, to increase an awareness of health and safety factors, and to create a basic understanding of the scientific method itself.

In social studies the unit used may become "a small part of living, a miniature society where the slow learner builds adjustive concepts of the social patterns he will meet in adult life." [25] Current events, topics of current interest related to school, home, and neighborhood, use of layman's reference materials, and the basic tools

---

[25] Metropolitan School Study Council, *The Slow Learner in the Average Classroom* (New York: The Council, 1954), p. 20.

and skills of reading and the other language arts are among the various ingredients of learning in the social studies areas. A specific device sometimes used is that of different texts and other reading materials that cover approximately the same topics, but which are adjusted to the varying abilities in a classroom.

As indicated earlier, the mentally dull are not always dull in the fields of art and music. Emphasis for slow learners in this direction is toward creating an ability to listen, to perform, to develop tastes, and to participate in interesting, enjoyable, and diverse activities. Through these outlets it is often possible to restore self-confidence and to provide a release for self-expression. Various art and music activities have also been used as a link with and motivation toward the other subject-matter areas.

Teaching Techniques

Many suggestions have been made regarding specific techniques that teachers of slow learners should use. The ones most frequently mentioned follow:

1. Simplify activities because these children cannot see as far ahead as others; shorten in length and narrow in scope.
2. Set up plans that are clear, definite, and precise.
3. Make relationships obvious.
4. Use demonstrations generously, making them concrete and tangible rather than verbal and abstract; include illustrations, audio-visual aids, field trips, and direct experiences.
5. Use drill and practice, but not meaningless rote or repetition; quantity without quality is futile.
6. Evaluate frequently and reassure often to help compensate for past frustrations, but give praise only if earned.
7. Develop "pride in outfit," in accomplishment, and in appearance.
8. Stress the practical and the immediately meaningful, such as current happenings at home, in school, in the community, and in world affairs.
9. Capitalize on individual abilities, such as those of an athletic, mechanical, social, artistic, or other nature; encourage creative ideas and interests or hobbies.
10. Refrain from undue pressures.
11. Use procedures that encourage student expression, includ-

ing teacher-pupil planning and group processes in classroom activities.

12. Seek and bring out vocational ambitions that are realistically founded.

It is probably obvious that references to vital and meaningful learning experiences are as appropriate for average and bright children as they are to slow learners. That is, of course, true. The necessity in all education for closely relating teaching techniques and the subject matter to be taught is vividly expressed in a thought-provoking statement made some years ago: "Greeting his pupils the master asked: What would you learn of me? And the reply came: How shall we care for our bodies? How shall we rear our children? How shall we work together? How shall we live with our fellowmen? How shall we play? For what ends shall we live? And the teacher pondered these words, and sorrow was in his heart, for his own learning touched not these things." [26]

Teaching techniques will necessarily be related to data garnered from identification and diagnostic sources. For children with specific learning disabilities, the pilot work of Cruickshank and his associates contains a wealth of specific classroom organization techniques and descriptions of teaching methods and curriculum used. The study demonstrated that structure and appropriate learning tasks were effective in creating successful experiences for children whose behavior was characteristic of brain-injured children, even when there could be no actual diagnosis made.

Current research relative to schedules of reinforcement and use of rewards and punishments need further translation into classroom practice and methodology. Team teaching is also increasingly discussed in the literature. An experiment at Flowing Wells School, Tucson, Arizona, describes an enthusiastic use of this innovation. In this plan, the leadership has been aware of a factor which is very important to the slow learner: the student's need for security that can come from close and consistent association with a specific teacher and group. In this case, the same group is maintained for language arts, social studies, and the special studies, but regrouping is done for science and mathematics. In five years, the school dis-

---

[26] J. C. Chapman and G. S. Counts, *Principles of Education* (Boston: Houghton Mifflin Company, 1924), p. ii.

trict has evolved from traditional to flexibly grouped elementary schools and has extended achievement grouping in the junior and senior high school by initiating a three-track program—basic, average, and honors—in all academic subjects.

On the basis of research and testing tenets of staff utilization in conjunction with team teaching, which have been made by Dr. Robert H. Anderson, Associate Professor, Graduate School of Education at Harvard University and J. Lloyd Trump, Associate Secretary of the National Association of Secondary School Principals, members of the Flowing Wells staff visited other school districts engaged in staff utilization projects. As a result of their observations and study, they identified a need for curriculum revision, individualized instruction, more effective staff utilization, and plants which would adequately incorporate the 20-25 per cent annually expanding school population.

Primary grades now have their 120 first or second grade students grouped together for instruction in science, mathematics, or social studies. Four homogeneous classes hear one lesson prepared by the teacher whose interest or strength could offer the best presentation. The three other teachers prepare material to follow the lesson; they use individualized instruction. A team planning center offers resource materials with teacher aides who assist in nonteaching duties.[27]

The extension of twentieth century technology into the teaching field in the form of programmed learning can offer some real assistance to help solve the educational problems of the slow learner. What is missing, of course, is the needed research to fill in existing gaps in our knowledge about individual differences and laws of learning. The following advantages, however, already exist in programmed instruction, so far as the needs of the slow learner are concerned:

1. The objectives or goals are clearly stated.
2. The steps in learning are specific and sequential.
3. The student participates actively in selecting answers.
4. The student is immediately reinforced for selecting the right answer.

[27] George Smith, *et al., "Team Teaching," Arizona Teacher* (November, 1961), pp. 20–24.

5. There is meaningful repetition and feed-back.

6. The student actively participates in the evaluation process and can identify his strengths and weaknesses.

Although adequately programmed materials are not plentifully available, the medium offers considerable promise for children who need the feeling of success that professionally prepared programmed instruction can provide. Teaching techniques, as well as educational content, in their application to the learning of slower students contain emphases worthy of special attention.

Cost Factor

An old source may set the pace for our thinking on the cost of educating slow learners: "Let all who question the wisdom of education for 'all the children' remember that America has not heretofore provided education for all as a gift from a strong, wealthy, and good people, but rather has become strong, wealthy, and good because education has been provided for all the people." [28] In reference to the cost of programs which attempt to increase services of the school, the 1960 White House Conference reported many suggestions for financial proposals related to "reassessment of local land values, broadening of the tax base, and increased Federal and State participation." [29]

Although it may be relatively simple to add up the expenses involved in special materials, equipment, guidance and teaching personnel, and administrative time, the problem becomes far more complex when one attempts to estimate the cost of *not* educating the slow learner. The cost to him, to his family, and to the society deprived of his maximal services can be less accurately measured, but it could be far greater if all elements of that loss could be totaled. Ingredients of it are in evasive factors such as voters without well-developed powers of reasoning, workers laboring below potential capability levels, consumers excessively gullible to catch-words and phrases, and taxpayers contributing far less than they would if their education had been more appropriately adapted to them.

---

[28] Hollingworth, *op. cit.*, p. 206.

[29] Betty Barton and Katharine D. Pringle, "Today's Children and Youth: As Viewed from the States," *Children,* Vol. 7, No. 2 (March-April, 1960), p. 55.

Educating slow learners may take time and energy that some feel might be used more profitably with other pupils. The use of public funds for them may be criticized. "And yet, if the American ideal of education for 'all the children of all the people' is ever going to be more than empty words, ways must be found to fit the school to the needs of the slow learners as effectively as to the needs of the more rapid learners." [30]

The Teacher

Who is a good teacher for slow-learning children? What are the characteristics of good teachers in general? What are the specific attributes of a good teacher? When one attempts to list the personal and professional qualities of capable teachers, the items accumulated take on a magnitude which is discouraging for the future teacher, unrealistic for the present one, and meaningless to the parent and child.

Abilities that contribute toward a sound learning situation with one child may hamper another. Personalities, physical settings, and parental and community attitudes are all factors to consider. In spite of the difficulties involved, however, there has been agreement on some of the qualities that most teachers of slow-learning children should possess. Many of their characteristics obviously overlap with those that all good teachers should have.

Their own knowledge of subject-matter areas, techniques of teaching them, stable physical and mental health, maturity, patience, and enthusiasm for working with slow learners should be on any such list. It is also necessary that they understand the techniques of child study and know how to interpret information related to child study. At least average intelligence of their own, and preferably a mental ability even higher than average, enters the picture. They must be able to adjust their expectations for children, adapting them to the lower levels of accomplishment expected of this group. The teacher should be able to conclude that the assignment of slow learners to his class is not in the realm of professional disciplining or discrimination against him; nor is it an unpleasant and inescap-

---

[30] Featherstone, *op. cit.*, p. viii.

able duty, but rather a chance to confront a difficult job with great built-in satisfactions.

A principle in child development is that people tend to behave as others expect them to behave. Likewise, the teacher who has faith and respect for individual achievement is known to have better results than the teacher who approached his slow-learning students with despair. Because such teaching is not an easy job, supervision needs to provide moral encouragement and support. Over-all goals and long-range objectives need to be evaluated so that administration and classroom practice are supportive and coordinated. The despair which teachers often experience because of the lack of referral services, as well as overwhelming individual needs, could be immeasurably helped by the use of a school social worker's skills. Teachers believed to be ineffective are often criticized, but they are not so often given the supportive assistance which would yield positive results from concentrated efforts.

Riessman states that teachers need two approaches: (1) Understand the child, and (2) understand the way subject matter can best be taught to him. If teachers are to be skillful at adapting for individual instruction, they need considerable training in the research and practice already garnered in areas of transfer of learning, motivation, and learning theory. Teachers need to have broad but well-defined goals in mind, so that they can move with confidence into individualized programs of instruction.

The teacher may be limited in his efforts because of class size, a shortage of specialized help, and a failure of his own background to include the specifics of "individual differences." In addition, a problem related to slow learning may be magnified if the teacher expects average work from below-average children, retains average standards, or uses the techniques of fear and punishment to create abilities that may be nonexistent. A vicious circle may evolve: The child is low and becomes lower because of the unrealistic pressures involved, and the lowering and pressuring continue.

The need for accepting people for what they are applies to the teacher of the slow learner. *Riessman makes a strong point of the need to stop underestimating the underprivileged.* Sources for change will in the end be more effective if they spring from the needs of the people involved. This requires that educators work with the other positive forces existing in the lives of the slow learner. It also means a focus different from that which traditional and subject-centered teachers have used as chief motivation for school success. It means building upon the positive values of the subcultures and minority groups. It means understanding the roots of prejudice and their corroding effects upon the slow learner. It means building respect for achievement. It means building upon the promising research which looks for recognition of creativity and for new ways of learning, as opposed to the traditional concepts of the way a fast-learning child should proceed. It means that the quality of education and its respect for democratic values must remain as the focus. This will take a reorientation of current attitudes toward the slow learner.

The problems related to educating these children accumulate within the classroom itself. It is there that many responsibilities crystallize. "Recognition and diagnosis of the causes of retarded academic achievement of individual children in the average classroom is the prime responsibility of the teacher in attempting to stimulate the maximum social, mental, and emotional growth and development of his pupils." [31]

---

[31] Metropolitan School Study Council, *op. cit.*, p. 1.

CHAPTER V

The Future

Much has been written about the slow learner, the causes of his learning handicaps, and ways to teach him. Therefore, many guidelines already exist in connection with improved educational programs.

Dugan, in an investigation of 105 tenth grade biology students as to their personal, social, educational, and economical reasons for success or lack of success in school, concluded: "Factors affecting lack of success in school today are very much the same as they were twenty years ago, in spite of economic prosperity, modifications in school curriculum, and increased school population. Further educational research is indicated with greater emphasis on *why* these are factors, rather than *what* the factors are." [1] Other writers put heavy emphasis on the increased severity of the problem today because of the many increased complexities in modern society. Equality of mankind does not imply equality of ability nor of the programs themselves. To assume so violates individuality, and it has been said many times in different ways that the resulting "humiliation and despair of chronic failure at prescribed tasks unsuited to capacity may be spared every child." [2]

In addition to the practices highlighted today by such experimental programs as Higher Horizons, Great Cities School Improvement Program, and the Community Talent Search, numerous other suggestions have been made for improving the educational accomplishments of slow learners. Among those most often mentioned are the following:

1. Use of the team approach and the involvement in diagnostic and teaching activities of as many specialists and others as necessary. In-

---

[1] Ruth Dugan, "An Investigation of the Personal, Social, Educational, and Economical Reasons for Success and Lack of Success in School as Expressed by 105 Tenth Grade Biology Students," *The Journal of Educational Research,* Vol. 55, No. 10 (August, 1962), pp. 544–53.

[2] Hollingworth, *op. cit.,* p. 210.

cluded are the parents, teachers, school administrators, guidance personnel, other specialized school personnel (health officer, social worker, psychometrist, psychologist), and, of course, the children themselves. Regarding the physical causes of slow learning (such as sight, hearing, and speech), a contribution might be made by a pediatrician, psychiatrist, neurologist, or other specialist. A trend has been noted toward increased interest and cooperation of professional personnel.

2. Cooperative research efforts in schools and communities, and with the involvement of state departments of education and universities, regarding educational programs, materials, and teaching techniques for slow learners. Other research needs are in areas such as parent and teacher attitudes toward slow learners; the contribution of vocational guidance and the importance of job placement; teacher preparation through preservice and in-service courses, workshops, institutes, and conferences; relationships among groups of children—slow learners, average, and above average; effects of class size on learning of slower students; deficiencies, accomplishments, and importance of public relation approaches to the problem; learning areas of greatest success; obstacles that block educational attainment; potentialities of programmed learning for these children.

3. Discovery of slow learning potential at early ages and the place of nursery schools and kindergartens in the educational framework. The slow learner should have a program planned to meet his individual learning problems from the time he enters school until the school considers him ready to function as a responsible member of the community. Programs which attempt suddenly to meet his special behavioral problems at the adolescent period have already missed the basic areas which typically begin with poor performance in academic skills.

4. Greater efforts toward individualized study of causes, needs, and suitable educational programs; adaptation of teaching materials and techniques; use of guidance personnel; review and modification of courses of study and subject content; realization that there is no single "best program" for slow learners.

5. The place of separating these children from the main educational stream for part of each day or week, or of a limited period of full separation during the first year or two of school to help increase readiness for various processes. A stronger trend, however, seems to be toward little or no educational separation of these children from other students.

6. Counseling and education of parents of slow learners.

7. Increased realization of community responsibilities.

8. Greater use of multiple methods of identification, rather than accepting the results of one test or opinion of one person; increased thoroughness of medical and psychological study.

9. Postponement in formal approaches to subject matter until readi-

ness patterns are developed to the extent that the slow learners can cope with them.

10. Supplementing the regular classroom teacher, on an itinerant or part-time basis, with another teacher who has had special preparation in remedial work.

11. Realization that the educational process is more than scholastic instruction. "It should encompass all feasible modes of preparation for life, living, and livelihood." [3]

12. Understanding that an improved school program for any group needing special help improves the program for all children, for the techniques are not new but merely adapted, and their use in one direction encourages individualized approaches in other directions.

A sound education for slow learners demands attention to the intelligence and understandings of adults as much as it does to the capabilities and limitations of children. What we accomplish in the future for these particular children depends upon how much we know about them and their needs and how conscientious we are in putting into practice or adapting, on at least an experimental basis, what some teachers, administrators, parents, and communities have already tried.

The comments of one writer in the field summarize our responsibility, as well as our opportunity, when he wrote:

> In school, at home, no matter where, one must never forget that the slow learner is no less a "person," no less an individual, than any other human being. His talents may be few, his promise slight, but he is none the less a member of mankind, cast in the same mold and made of the same clay. He claims equal rights with others in the regard of his fellow men, and to guidance and instruction designed to stimulate his growth to the fullest stature his powers permit. He too must be helped to stand on his own feet and face the world, self-reliant and unafraid. "With malice towards none, with charity for all" must be the teacher's watchword. Any other point of view denies the faith that has made America great. [4]

---

[3] Doll, *op. cit.*, p. 86.
[4] Featherstone, *op. cit.*, p. 118.

Bibliography

Abraham, Willard, *A New Look at Reading*. Boston: Porter Sargent, 1956.

———, "These Kinds of Mental Retardation are Preventable," *Midwest Magazine* (September 17, 1961).

Allingham, R. Bruce and George W. Connelly, "What Are Secondary Schools Doing to Develop A Program for the Slow Learner?" *Bulletin of the National Association of Secondary-School Principals,* Vol. 40, No. 219 (April, 1956), pp. 261–63.

Almy, Millie, *Ways of Studying Children*. New York: Bureau of Publications, Teachers College, Columbia University, 1959.

American Council on Education, *Helping Teachers Understand Children*. Washington, D.C.: The Council, 1945.

American Educational Research Association, *Review of Educational Research*, Vol. XXIX, No. 5. Washington, D.C.: National Education Association, 1959.

Arizona State University, *Investigation of Mental Retardation and Pseudo-Mental Retardation in Relation to Bilingual and Sub-Cultural Factors.* Tempe, Ariz.: The University, 1960.

Baker, Harry J., *Introduction to Exceptional Children*. New York: The Macmillan Company, 1959.

Birch, Jack W., "Exceptional Children in Your Regular Classroom," *Grade Teacher,* Vol. LXXV, No. 7 (March, 1958), pp. 34–35, 90–91.

Blaha, M. Jay, "Meeting Individual Differences," *Bulletin of the National Association of Secondary-School Principals,* Vol. 34, No. 174 (December, 1950), pp. 97–108.

Blair, Glenn Myers, *Mentally Superior and Inferior Children in the Junior and Senior High School*. New York: Bureau of Publications, Teachers College, Columbia University, 1938.

Bloom, Irving and Walter I. Murray, "Some Basic Issues in Teaching Slow Learners," *Understanding the Child,* Vol. XXVI, No. 3 (June, 1957), pp. 85–91.

Boggs, Elizabeth, "Mongolism, New Discoveries Every Month," *Children Limited* (April, 1962), pp. 6–9.

Bond, Guy L. and Miles Tinker, *Reading Difficulties: Their Diagnosis and Correction*. New York: Appleton-Century-Crofts, Inc., 1957.

Buhler, Charlotte, Faith Smitter, and Sybil Richardson, *Childhood Problems and the Teacher*. New York: Holt, Rinehart & Winston, Inc., 1952.

Burt, Cyril, *The Causes and Treatment of Backwardness*. New York: Philosophical Library, Inc., 1953.

Caplan, Gerald, ed., *Prevention of Mental Disorders in Children*. New York: Basic Books, Inc., 1961.

Chapman, J. C. and G. S. Counts, *Principles of Education*. Boston: Houghton Mifflin Company, 1924.

Cheshire Education Committee, *The Education of Dull Children at the Primary Stage*. London: University of London Press, 1956.

Clark, Margaret M., *Teaching Left-Handed Children*. New York: Philosophical Library, Inc., 1961.

Cleugh, M. F., ed., *Teaching the Slow Learner in the Special School*. New York: Philosophical Library, Inc., 1961.

Cleugh, M. F., *The Slow Learner, Some Educational Principles and Policies*. New York: Philosophical Library, Inc., 1957.

Clemmens, Raymond L., M.D., "Minimal Brain Damage in Children," *Children,* Vol. 8, No. 5 (September-October, 1961), pp. 179–84.

Cohen, Eli E. and Louise Kapp, "Youth and Work: The Second Challenge," *Children,* Vol. 9, No. 2 (March-April, 1962), pp. 79–83.

Collett, Robert W., M.D., "We're Winning the War on Mental Retardation," *This Week Magazine* (October 21, 1962).

Conant, James B., *Slums and Suburbs*. New York: McGraw-Hill, Inc., 1961.
———, "Social Dynamite in Our Large Cities," *Children,* Vol. 8, No. 5 (September-October, 1961), pp. 163–69.

Conklin, Agnes M., *Failures of Highly Intelligent Pupils*. New York: Bureau of Publications, Teachers College, Columbia University, 1940.

Cruickshank, William M. and G. Orville Johnson, eds., *Education of Exceptional Children and Youth*. Englewood Cliffs, N.J.: Prentice-Hall, Inc., 1958.

Cruickshank, William M., et al., *A Teaching Method for Brain-Injured and Hyperactive Children*. Syracuse, N.Y.: Syracuse University Press, 1961.

Davidson, Helen P., "An Experimental Study of Bright, Average, and Dull Children at the Four-Year Mental Level," *Genetic Psychology Monographs,* Vol. IX, No.'s 3–4 (March-April, 1931).

DeHaan, Robert F. and Jack Kough, *Helping Children With Special Needs,* Elementary School Edition, Vol. II. Chicago: Science Research Associates, 1956.

Detroit Board of Education, Report: "Great Cities Program for School Improvement in Areas Where Pupils Have Limited Backgrounds," October 22, 1960.

D'Evelyn, Katherine E., *Individual Parent-Teacher Conferences: A Manual for Teachers of Young Children*. New York: Bureau of Publications, Teachers College, Columbia University, 1959.

Dillon, Harold J., *Early School Leavers, A Major Educational Problem*. New York: National Child Labor Committee, 1949.

Dodds, B. L., "What is a Good Program for the Slow Learner?" *Bulletin of the National Association of Secondary-School Principals,* Vol. 36, No. 185 (March, 1952), pp. 329–33.

Dolch, Edward William, *Helping Handicapped Children in School.* Champaign, Ill.: Garrard Press, 1948.

Doll, Edgar A., "Varieties of Slow Learners," *Exceptional Children,* Vol. 20, No. 2 (November, 1953), pp. 61–64, 86.

Driscoll, Gertrude, *How To Study the Behavior of Children.* New York: Bureau of Publications, Teachers College, Columbia University, 1941.

Dugan, Ruth, "An Investigation of the Personal, Social, Educational, and Economical Reasons for Success and Lack of Success in School as Expressed by 105 Tenth Grade Biology Students," *The Journal of Educational Research,* Vol. 55, No. 10 (August, 1962), pp. 544–53.

Eagles, Eldon L., M.D., "Health Research," *Children,* Vol. 8, No. 5 (September-October, 1961), p. 195.

Eames, Thomas H., "Some Neural and Glandular Bases of Learning," *Journal of Education,* Boston University, Vol. 142, No. 4 (April, 1960).

Educational Policies Commission, *Education and the Disadvantaged American.* Washington, D.C.: National Education Association, 1962.

Edwards, Rosaline M., "A Slow Learner Program," *Bulletin of the National Association of Secondary-School Principals,* Vol. 42, No. 235 (February, 1958), pp. 130–32.

Eisman, Louis, "The Slow Learner Is Here to Stay," *High Points,* Vol. XXXV, No. 1 (January, 1953), pp. 10–15.

Featherstone, W. B., *Teaching the Slow Learner.* New York: Bureau of Publications, Teachers College, Columbia University, 1941.

Flato, Charles, "Parents Who Beat Children," *Saturday Evening Post* (October 6, 1962), pp. 30–35.

Frain, Thomas J., *Administrative and Instructional Provisions for Rapid and Slow Learners in Catholic Secondary Schools.* Washington, D.C.: The Catholic University of America Press, 1956.

Frandsen, Arden N., *How Children Learn.* New York: McGraw-Hill, Inc., 1957.

Gallagher, James J., *The Tutoring of Brain-Injured Mentally Retarded Children.* Springfield, Ill.: Charles C. Thomas, Publisher, 1960.

Gates, Arthur I. and Miriam C. Pritchard, *Teaching Reading to Slow-Learning Pupils.* New York: Bureau of Publications, Teachers College, Columbia University, 1942.

Ginzberg, Eli, *Human Resources: The Wealth of a Nation.* New York: Simon and Schuster, Inc., 1958.

Hecker, Stanley E., "Early School Leavers in Kentucky," *Bulletin of the Bureau of School Service,* Vol. XXV, No. 4 (June, 1953). Lexington, Ky.: College of Education, University of Kentucky.

Heffernan, Helen, "Evaluation More Than Testing," in *Readings in Educational Psychology,* eds. Victor H. Noll and Rachel P. Noll. New York: The Macmillan Company, 1962.

Heiser, Karl F., *Our Backward Children*. New York: W. W. Norton & Company, Inc., 1955.

Hollingworth, Leta, *Special Talents and Defects*. New York: The Macmillan Company, 1923.

Holt, Charles C. and Owen M. Henson, "How Can the School Best Provide for the Slow Learner?" *Bulletin of the National Association of Secondary-School Principals*, Vol. 41, No. 228 (April, 1957), pp. 162–65.

Huffman, Mildred Blake, *Fun Comes First for Blind Slow Learners*. Springfield, Ill.: Charles C. Thomas, Publisher, 1957.

Hull, J. Dan and Howard H. Cummings, "How Fare American Youth in 1962?" *School Life*, Vol. 44, No. 4 (January-February, 1962), pp. 13–16.

Hunter, Marjorie, "Plan for Retarded Given to President," *The New York Times*, Western Edition, October 16, 1962.

Ingram, Christine P., *Education of the Slow-Learning Child*. New York: The Ronald Press Company, 1960.

Jerome, Sister Agnes, "A Study of Twenty Slow Learners," *Journal of Educational Research*, Vol. 53, No. 1 (September, 1959), pp. 23–27.

Jewett, Arno and J. Dan Hull, coordinators, *Teaching Rapid and Slow Learners in High Schools*, U.S. Department of Health, Education, and Welfare Bulletin No. 5, 1954; reprinted 1957, 1960.

Johnson, G. Orville, *Education For the Slow Learners*. Englewood Cliffs, N.J.: Prentice-Hall, Inc., 1963.

———, "The Slow Learner—A Second-Class Citizen?" The J. Richard Street Lecture for 1962, Syracuse University, Syracuse, N.Y.

Keim, Edwin B. and Carl F. Hansen, "How Can the School Best Provide for the Slow Learner?" *Bulletin of the National Association of Secondary-School Principals*, Vol. 41, No. 228 (April, 1957), pp. 77–81.

Kirk, Samuel A., *Early Education of the Mentally Retarded*. Urbana, Ill.: The University of Illinois Press, 1960.

———, *Teaching Reading to Slow-Learning Children*. Boston: Houghton Mifflin Company, 1940.

Kirk, Samuel A. and G. Orville Johnson, *Educating the Retarded Child*. Boston: Houghton Mifflin Company, 1961.

Kirk, Samuel A., Merle B. Karnes, and Winifred D. Kirk, *You and Your Retarded Child*. New York: The Macmillan Company, 1955.

Kirk, Samuel A. and Oliver P. Kolstoe, "The Mentally Retarded," *Review of Educational Research*, Vol. XXIII, No. 5 (December, 1953), pp. 400–416.

Kough, Jack and Robert F. DeHaan, *Identifying Children With Special Needs*, Elementary School Edition, Vol. I. Chicago: Science Research Associates, 1955.

Kvaraceus, William C., "The Delinquent," *Review of Educational Research*, Vol. XXIX, No. 5 (December, 1959), pp. 545–52.

Langdon, Grace and Irving W. Stout, *Parent-Teacher Relationships*, Research Bulletin 16, American Educational Research Association, National Education Association, 1958.

Lee, J. Murray and Dorris May Lee, *The Child and His Development*. New York: Appleton-Century-Crofts, Inc., 1958.

Levy, Nissim M. and Joseph M. Cuddy, "Concept Learning in the Educationally Retarded Child of Normal Intelligence," *Journal of Consulting Psychology*, Vol. 20, No. 6 (December, 1956), pp. 445–48.

Lightfoot, Georgia, *Personality Characteristics of Bright and Dull Children*. New York: Bureau of Publications, Teachers College, Columbia University, 1951.

Lloyd, Frances, *Educating the Sub-Normal Child*. New York: Philosophical Library, Inc., 1953.

Martin, William E. and Celia Burns Stendler, *Child Behavior and Development*. New York: Harcourt, Brace & World, Inc., 1959.

Masland, Richard L., Seymour B. Sarason, and Thomas Gladwin, *Mental Subnormality*. New York: Basic Books, Inc., 1960.

McCarthy, Agnes, "Teaching Slow Learners to Write," *Bulletin of the National Association of Secondary-School Principals*, Vol. 39, No. 212 (September, 1955), pp. 106–10.

McClelland, D. C., *et al.*, *Talent and Society*, Princeton, N.J.: D. Van Nostrand Co., Inc., 1958.

McKenna, Bernard H., "Greater Learning in Smaller Classes," *NEA Journal* (October, 1957), pp. 437–38.

———, "What About Class Size?" *New York State Education*, Vol. XLV, No. 2 (November, 1957), pp. 99–101.

McLoughlin, W. P., "Class Size Affects Learning Ability," *School Executive*, Vol. 75 (March, 1956), pp. 91–93.

Metropolitan School Study Council, *The Slow Learner in the Average Classroom*. New York: The Council, 1954.

Morrison, Ida E. and Ida F. Perry, "Acceptance of Overage Children by Their Classmates," *Elementary School Journal*, Vol. LVI, No. 5 (January, 1956), pp. 217–20.

Murphy, Lois Barclay, *The Widening World of Childhood*. New York: Basic Books, Inc., 1962.

National Education Association, *Project on the Academically Talented Student*. Washington, D.C.: The Association, 1959.

National Education Association Research Division, "Best Class Size," *NEA Research Bulletin*, Vol. 39, No. 4 (December, 1961), p. 107.

———, "High School Methods With Slow Learners," *Research Bulletin of the National Educational Association*, Vol. 21, No. 3, October, 1943, pp. 59–87.

National Society for the Study of Education, *The Education of Exceptional Children*, 49th Yearbook, Part II, Chapter XIII, Elizabeth M. Kelly and Harvey A. Stevens, "Special Education for the Mentally Handicapped." Chicago: The Society, 1950.

New England School Development Council, *Some Basic Educational Principles and Their Applications in Early Adolesence.* Cambridge, Mass.: Spaulding House, 1956.

Nickel, Kenneth N., "Better Education for Nonacademic Pupils," *North Central Association Quarterly,* Vol. XXXI, No. 4 (April, 1957), pp. 352–84.

Niemeyer, John H., "Splitting the Social Atom," *Saturday Review* (September 12, 1959).

Passow, A. Harry, Jane E. Beasley, and Deton J. Brooks, Jr., "Adapting the Curriculum to the Needs, Capabilities, and Talents of Individual Students," *Review of Educational Research,* Vol. XXVII, No. 3 (June, 1957), pp. 277–86.

Pauling, Linus, "Inheriting Bad Health," *Time Magazine* (February 2, 1962), p. 37.

Peck, John R., "The Status of the Retarded Learner," *High School Journal,* Vol. 36, No. 6 (March, 1953), pp. 179–84.

Pellmann, Maurine and G. P. Liddle, "A Program for the Problem Child," *Phi Delta Kappan* (January, 1959), pp. 174–78.

Penfield, W., "The Interpretive Cortex," *Science,* Vol. 129 (June 26, 1959), pp. 1719–25.

Plato, *The Republic of Plato,* trans. F. M. Cornford. New York: Oxford University Press, 1954.

Portenier, Lillian G., *Pupils of Low Mentality in High School.* New York: Bureau of Publications, Teachers College, Columbia University, 1933.

Riessman, Frank, *The Culturally Deprived Child.* New York: Harper & Row, Publishers, 1962.

Rosenberger, Homer Tope, "Assistance for the Slow Learner," *Bulletin of the National Association of Secondary-School Principals,* Vol. 40, No. 217 (February, 1956), pp. 128–36.

Sandusky, Annie Lee, "Services to Neglected Children," *Children,* Vol. 7, No. 1 (January-February, 1960), pp. 23–28.

Sanford, Edna G., "The Bright Child Who Fails," *Understanding the Child,* Vol. XXI, No. 3 (June, 1952), pp. 85–88.

Savoy, Maggie, "Careers for Youth Finds a Way," news article in *The Arizona Republic,* April 8, 1962.

Schmidt, Frances and Mildred I. French, "White House Conference Follow-up Within the States," *Children,* Vol. 9, No. 1 (January-February, 1962), pp. 3–8.

Sexton, Patricia Cayo, *Education and Income.* New York: The Viking Press, Inc., 1961.

Smith, George, *et al.,* "Team Teaching," *Arizona Teacher* (November, 1961), pp. 20–24.

Smith, Henry P. and Emerald V. Dechant, *Psychology in Teaching Reading.* Englewood Cliffs, N.J.: Prentice-Hall, Inc., 1961.

Smith, Marion Funk, *Teaching the Slow Learning Child.* New York: Harper & Row, Publishers, 1954.

Strang, Ruth, *An Introduction to Child Study.* New York: The Macmillan Company, 1959.

———, "Intellectual Differences," *Childhood Education,* Vol. 32, No. 5 (January, 1956), pp. 211–14.

———, *Reporting to Parents.* New York: Bureau of Publications, Teachers College, Columbia University, 1958.

Stratemeyer, Florence B., Hamden L. Forkner, and Margaret G. McKim, *Developing a Curriculum for Modern Living.* New York: Bureau of Publications, Teachers College, Columbia University, 1947.

Sullivan, Helen Blair, "Teaching the Slow Learner," *NEA Journal,* Vol. 40, No. 2 (February, 1951), pp. 115–16.

Symonds, Percival M., *What Education Has to Learn from Psychology.* New York: Bureau of Publications, Teachers College, Columbia University, 1958.

Tansley, A. E. and R. Gulliford, *The Education of Slow Learning Children.* London: Routledge & Kegan Paul, Ltd., 1960.

Taylor, James L., Lillian L. Gore, and Hazel F. Gabbard, *Functional Schools for Young Children,* United States Department of Health, Education, and Welfare Bulletin OE-21006, Special Publication No. 8. Washington, D.C.: Government Printing Office, 1961.

Taylor, Katherine Whiteside, "A Community-Wide Program of Parent Education," *Children,* Vol. 9, No. 1 (January-February, 1962), pp. 9–14.

Torgerson, Theodore L., *Studying Children.* New York: Dryden Press, 1947.

Tucker, Ruel E., "A Program for Slow Learners," *Bulletin of the National Association of Secondary-School Principals,* Vol. 36, No. 185 (March, 1952), pp. 333–36.

United States Senate, Committee on Labor and Public Welfare, Subcommittee on Education, *Educational Assistance to Migrant Agricultural Employees and Their Children.* Washington, D.C.: Government Printing Office, 1960.

United States Department of Health, Education, and Welfare, *Distributive Education, A Study of Curriculum Development in the High School Cooperative Program,* OE-82000. Washington, D.C.: Government Printing Office, 1960.

United States Office of Education, *Teaching Rapid and Slow Learners in High School.* Washington, D.C.: Government Printing Office, 1954.

Walsh, Ann Marie, *Self Concepts of Bright Boys With Learning Difficulties.* New York: Bureau of Publications, Teachers College, Columbia University, 1956.

White, Verna, *Studying the Individual Pupil.* New York: Harper & Row, Publishers, 1958.

White House Conference on Children and Youth, *Reference Papers on Children and Youth.* Washington, D.C.: Government Printing Office, 1960.

Wilson, Frank T., "A Comparison of Difficulty and Improvement in the

Learning of Bright and Dull Children in Reproducing a Descriptive Selection," *Genetic Psychology Monographs*, Vol. IX, No. 6 (June), 1931.

————, *Learning of Bright and Dull Children*. New York: Bureau of Publications, Teachers College, Columbia University, 1928.

Case Study

The following composite case study has been taken from the research project *Investigation of Mental Retardation and Pseudo Mental Retardation in Relation to Bilingual and Sub-Cultural Factors*.[1] No real names have been used and no basic details have been altered. It is a living example of a type of "slow learning" and an insight into some of the reasons for it.

Consuela Moreno

A house consisting of two small rooms and made of scrap lumber, with no electricity, no water, no toilet facilities, no heating, no cooling, with large cracks in the walls through which summer heat, winter cold, rain, and dust blow freely—this is where Consuela Moreno lives with her family of two adults and seven children. Inside the house are a bed, an old dining room table, boxes used as cupboards, foods, and a kerosene lamp. Behind the house is another small structure, a flimsy shelter made of scrap wood and old sheets, bedspreads, and canvas, where four additional beds are located. Also nearby are two outhouses shared by neighbors and patrons of the bar located in front of the house. The one water tap in the yard is also shared with many others.

The broader setting includes the bar, an automobile repair shop, and some industrial property. It also includes the only play space for children—some vacant land covered with bits of glass, tin cans, other small trash, and deep ruts filled with fine pulverized dirt that becomes mud in rainy weather. There are no trees, flowers, grass, toys, or play equipment. Traffic is very heavy on both nearby streets.

---

[1] Arizona State University, *Investigation of Mental Retardation and Pseudo-Mental Retardation in Relation to Bilingual and Sub-Cultural Factors* (Tempe, Ariz.: University Bookstore, Arizona State University, 1960). Research performed pursuant to a contract with the United States Department of Health, Education, and Welfare.

From this home and neighborhood Consuela goes to school, and she seldom misses a day. Even on cold, winter days she wears a sleeveless pinafore pinned together in the back where buttons belong, and without socks and underwear. Her clothing is invariably of poor quality and ill-fitting. She is usually dirty, and is undoubtedly the most poorly dressed child in her classroom.

But there are striking contrasts between her environment and superficial outward appearance—and the person she probably really is. Let us look at her more closely.

Consuela is almost plump, has even, attractive features, and most of the time has a placid, pleasant expression. Beneath the surface is enjoyment of beauty, rhythm, and animation. One day she went with her class to see Christmas decorations in a large shopping center. At one point they all stopped to watch an exhibition of "The Dancing Waters," where the water was controlled and made to conform to the rhythm of music. Consuela was fascinated, and as the music continued, she kept time with it and imitated the movements of the changing moods and rhythms of the water. She was completely oblivious to everything and everybody around her, although her own absorption and enjoyment were so keen that they drew the attention of many adults and children near her.

Her agility, gracefulness, and quick reactions are among many of Consuela's affirmative attributes. She writes and draws with ease, has only a slight accent, has progressed steadily in school, and seems secure in her relationships with other children. In some play activities at school she shows a leadership quality. At the end of second grade her reading test grade was 3.2.

Consuela scored slightly below average on her two individual intelligence tests, 86 on the WISC and 81 on the Arthur Point Scale. In connection with the latter test the psychometrist noted, "The spread of scores might indicate that this IQ is an underestimate of her ability."

Here may be a true case of pseudo mental retardation, or at least pseudo slow learning, of a child from one of the poorest home environments in the entire study.

Consuela is the oldest of the seven children. Her step-father is her mother's common law husband, and is the real father of her four younger sisters. The father of Consuela and the other two children deserted the family in Idaho in 1953, and has not been heard from since.

Mrs. Guerra and her first husband followed the crops as her parents had done before them since coming to the United States from Mexico, in 1937. She and Mr. Guerra, her present husband, continued to do so for a while, until they came to their present location in 1955, where all four younger children of this union have been born. Mr. Guerra picks cotton, and his earnings are irregular, depending on crop conditions.

Their house rental is $10.00 a month. Although Mrs. Guerra recognizes the inadequacies of their present housing, she anticipates no change in the future. She stated that sometimes it is so cold that the family spends the entire day in bed. There is an ordinance against building a fire outside, but once in a while the family does anyway, in the early winter mornings. Other times it is so hot that it is impossible to stay inside, so they go outdoors and follow the shade from the house as the day progresses, sleeping outside at night.

Mrs. Guerra's parents live in Texas where they have lived for many years. Her father who recently visited her hadn't seen her for eight years. He was very upset with the way she and her family lived, saying, "This isn't even good enough for chickens." Mrs. Guerra once nostalgically commented that the old days in a labor camp in Idaho were much better, for then each family was furnished with a wood-burning stove.

They did receive an application form for a housing project, but she felt it probably had been lost. They never bought any furniture because it would be impossible to keep up the payments. Charity provided the few possessions they now have.

The limited, uneven earnings are doled out to Mrs. Guerra on a daily basis for food purchases, and no food is bought in advance. Their diet consists largely of meat and beans, and there are no vegetables (because Mr. Guerra doesn't like them) and no chicken (because of the inadequate cooking facilities). Mrs. Guerra would like to have more responsibility for handling money, and feels that her husband's control of it is one reason why they have such poor housing. He spends money on sweets and other nonessentials, she said, and when he takes the children into the cotton fields he buys them hamburgers and pop.

The family has no fun together as a group. They have no money, no transportation, belong to no clubs or organizations. Even a radio they once had no longer belongs to them, and without electricity a television set would do no good. Consuela's mother wistfully mentioned that she would like to take her family to the country sometimes, but had no means of getting there.

Parental hopes for their children are beyond expectations. High school and secretarial jobs are among the hopes, but they are tempered by the realization that "free education" is not really free, that books cost money, and that possible later incomes from the older children would have to be sacrificed if they were to continue beyond elementary school. Mrs. Guerra is far from certain that they will even complete eight grades.

Consuela has already helped indirectly with the family earnings. She has gone with her father to the cotton fields and carried water, thus saving him the time he would lose if she were not there.

Consuela's early development was normal—full-term baby, nursed until a year old, walking at 15 months. Her early childhood has been comparatively healthy. Her medical records show no innoculations of any kind until she was seven years old.

Evaluations by her teachers indicate parts of her personality not revealed from other sources. Occasional disruptiveness and aggressiveness in class are attributed to her desire to be noticed, to participate, to be active even when she may not be capable of performing adequately. She draws attention to how helpful she is to others, showing an eagerness to be praised. Her enjoyment of school was commented upon, and so was her intelligence as being average or even slightly above average.

It is interesting to note that in all of the home visits made by the social worker, Consuela's step-father was never present even though appointments were made on the basis of his free time after work. One teacher referred to his drinking, although his wife never did.

Spanish is the dominant language in the home, the one which is most frequently spoken to the children. However, Mrs. Guerra says she is making more of an effort to speak English to the younger ones because she would like them to learn it before they go to school. She had about six years of schooling but only completed third grade.

Her present husband told her he had finished eighth grade, but he does not speak English very well, she said.

She feels the school is doing a good job with her children, three of whom are now in school. The second child, a girl, seems to be having difficulty in first grade because she cannot understand the material given to her; all of their scolding apparently does no good, they feel.

The family's cultural ties, holidays, and food are closely aligned with Mexico. However, there are no indications in the home through decorative or printed materials that activities are dominated in any way from either a cultural or educational direction. The activities and products of learning are completely absent.

Both parents like this area, according to the mother, but dislike their neighborhood. She expressed her fear of colored people, and especially of the ones who frequent the bar near their house and use their toilet facilities. She doesn't like what they say, and doesn't want them near her children. However, at present there are no plans to move.

So Consuela Moreno will no doubt stay where she is, be cold in the winter, hot in the summer, and subjected to all the limitations of a barren home and neighborhood environment. Even with these she appears to be on the intellectual fringe of the average. With an environment that would stimulate, that would open doors of cultural breadth and growth possibilities, her intellectual borders might be able to expand outward. But currently there is no hope, not even a flicker of one, that the future will provide opportunities any more plentifully than have the past or the present.

The Education of the Slow Learner in the Mesa, Arizona, Public Schools[1]

In 1952–53, the Mesa Public Schools embarked on a program of identifying the exceptional child. However, it was not until the introduction of a new method of reporting test scores that the programs for the slow learner were made feasible. In 1959–60, the method of reporting achievement scores in terms of grade placement and intelligence scores in terms of I.Q. was replaced with the concept of a "Stanine" or standard of nine. This method made immediate comparison of the student's ability and achievement possible. It was in terms, also, that the teacher could understand. The stanine is a standard of nine which is directly related to the Normal Curve. The Normal Curve is divided into nine parts to correspond to the standard deviation. The stanine of 5 is average and represents a band of scores from a $-.25\sigma$ to a $+.25\sigma$. The stanine of 1 is low and the 9 is high. A difference of 3 between two stanine scores is significant at the one per cent level of confidence.

Since 1952–53 the Mesa Public Schools have had a standardized testing program for intelligence, achievement, and aptitude. The California Test of Mental Maturity, Short Form, has been used to survey intelligence in grades 2, 4, 6, 8, and 10. The Metropolitan Reading Readiness Test has been used on the first grade level to ascertain reading readiness. The Gates Primary reading test has been used at the beginning of the second grade and the Gates Advanced Primary reading test has been used at the end of the second grade to determine reading ability and advancement on the second grade level. The California Achievement test has been used on all other grade levels—3 to 10—to survey achievement status.

Until the year 1960–61, no organized plan for the education of

---

[1] By Dr. David O. Lloyd, Director of Guidance and Special Services, Mesa Public Schools, Mesa, Arizona.

the slow learner had been in existence in the Mesa Public Schools. There had been, however, two classes established for the mentally retarded students who were in the educable category, that is, with an I.Q. ranging approximately from 55 to 75.

In 1960–61 three schools, hereafter designated Schools *A, B,* and *C,* adopted programs for the education of the slow, average, and superior student. These range from School *A,* which grouped at only one grade level, to School *C,* which grouped its entire student body. All three schools grouped according to reading ability. The three programs will be treated separately, as they were developed independently of each other.

School A

School *A* has grouped its second grade classes into three levels (low, average, and superior) and into four classes. The purpose for grouping was to see whether (1) the students who had not found success in the first grade could be helped to achieve success in the second grade, (2) more help could be given to individual problems, and (3) a psychological feeling of success in school and school activities could be provided. It was hoped that the children who were slow learners could be brought up to their regular grade level by the end of the school year, and thus could go into the regular third grade class and achieve successfully.

How the students were identified. The students in the low achievers' section were selected on the basis of their past performance and potential for success as recommended by the first grade teacher. Performance on the Gates Reading Readiness Test, Primary Form, was utilized, as well as the intelligence test results on the California Test of Mental Maturity, Short Form.

An analysis of class test results showed that two, or 9.5 per cent, fell into the third stanine; one, or 4.8 per cent, fell into the fourth stanine; three, or 15 per cent, fell into the fifth stanine; seven, or 33 per cent, fell into the sixth stanine; four, or 19 per cent, fell in the seventh stanine; three, or 14 per cent, fell in the eighth stanine; one, or 4.8 per cent, fell in the ninth stanine.

Teachers' observations were based solely on the student's ability to read. At the beginning of the school year the second grade teacher added to this class a few students who appeared to be low in reading ability. A number of these children, based on teacher opinion, would have been retained in first grade. At the start of the school year there were 18 in the class, but by the end of the second week there were 22. The class had as high as 26 for a short period of time, but the class average was 23.

The program. The class adopted the *Phonetic Keys to Reading Program,* published by the Economy Company. The class as a whole went back into first grade reading materials; however, they did not use the same books. Many supplementary texts were utilized, and these texts were based on individual teacher choice. No form of spelling was taught during the first twelve weeks, or until after the alphabet had been thoroughly covered. The second grade arithmetic book was used, but at a slow pace. The second grade social studies units were used, but in a more simple form.

Results at the end of the seventh month. Of the 23 children, four had improved to the point where they would be able to do third grade work. Five had progressed to the point where they would be able to go on into the third grade but would probably have to review most of the second grade material. Five were to be promoted to the third grade on the basis of social promotion, due to their low mental ability. Nine children were considered for retention, but next year would be placed in a normal second grade; all nine had mental ability of average or above, but did not achieve to the desired second grade level. These nine were making progress on a first grade basis but were not making progress commensurate with their ability. They seemed to lack interest, desire, and initiative. They would do the assigned tasks but make no attempt to go beyond. All of the students in the class made a decided improvement in their study habits and attitude, that is, from varying degrees of dislike to one of acceptance.

School B

In School *B,* three grade levels were grouped—grades 1, 2, and 3—according to reading ability. In the first and second grades, there were four classes each. One class was very low, one slightly below average, one slightly above average, and one superior. In the third grade there were three classes, grouped low, average, and superior.

How the students were identified. On the first grade level the students were grouped on the basis of the results of the Metropolitan Reading Readiness Test. On the second grade level they were grouped according to the opinions of the first grade teacher and the results of a two weeks' trial period at the beginning of the school year. The third grade was grouped on the basis of the opinions of the previous teacher and the results of the Gates Primary reading test, which had been administered both in the fall and the spring, and on the California Test of Mental Maturity results.

On the second and third grade level, where the student had not been in the system the previous year, report card and other identifying information was used to place the student.

Results at the end of the seventh month. In the low group a great deal of attention was given to phonics and reading fundamentals. On the first grade level the low group was made up of many non-English speaking students who came from an impoverished environment (many were from a transient farm population). Many supplementary texts were used and much explanation was required. The results, based on teacher observation, seem to be that many students were profiting from the type of program offered.

School C

School *C* had 23 classes, all of which were grouped according to reading ability in grades 1 through 6. This was the most ambitious program for the low achiever that had been yet attempted in the Mesa Schools. The basic philosophy of the program was that many children who were slow learners failed to read because they met more severe competition than they were able to cope with and that because of this competition they tended to give up rather than attempt to meet the challenges. Another part of the philosophy was that when the range of ability was reduced, the slow learner would experience successful achievement and have greater academic success.

How the students were identified. The following four steps applied to all grade levels.

1. The students on each grade level were first ranked according

to the results of standardized tests in terms of reading ability. On the first grade level the test used was the Metropolitan Reading Readiness Test. The second grade used the Gates Primary and Advanced Reading tests. The third through sixth used the California Achievement Tests. No attention was paid at this point to the student's intellectual ability. The superior student was ranked top and the low student was ranked at the bottom. This ranking was made in the spring of the year before school was dismissed for summer vacation.

2. The low group was then selected from the bottom and the high group from the top, and the remainder were divided into the remaining classes. The class size was determined by the following formula: the low group was limited in size to 10 students below that of the regular room. The top group had the regular room population plus three.

3. An evaluation sheet was filled out by the current year's teacher on each student in her room.

4. She then met with the next year's teacher and they adjusted the ranking on the basis of their own evaluation. They took into consideration, also, the behavioral and social adjustment of the individual.

At the writing of this report, the first and second grades were grouped so that there was one low class, one near-low class, two average classes, and one high class. The third grade had one low, one slightly below average, one slightly above average, and one superior class. In the fourth to sixth grade, on each grade level, there was one low class, one average class, and one superior class.

Results at the end of the seventh month. This program was devised with the help of the teachers and found wide acceptance among them. After seven months they found that where in the beginning the low students were all approximately the same in reading achievement, at the end of the seven months there was a wide spread in achievement. For example, eight in the third grade who were in the low group reached the reading level of the average of the third grade at the end of seven months, and were scheduled to be promoted to the regular class next year.

In the fourth grade there was a great deal of interest shown on the part of the parents and students. In the sixth grade where the low class was made up almost entirely of boys (there were only three girls), high interest was demonstrated in the field of science; at the beginning of the year, the teacher attempted to stimulate this interest by utilizing the *My Weekly Reader Science* booklets. The grade level at the beginning of the year averaged approximately 2.2 in reading ability. After 27 weeks of school the majority of these students reached the level of the regular sixth grade reading books. They started at the second grade level in the *My Weekly Reader Science* series, went through the fifth grade level in the same series, then went into the fourth grade *Paths to Follow Golden Rule* series, and then progressed to the fifth grade level in the Scott Foresman *Peoples and Progress* series. The low second grade class won first prize in the second grade division at the district science fair.

Problems Related to These Programs

1. Universally the teachers in the slower groups have miscalculated in what the low class would be able to accomplish. These programs need much enriched materials. The lack of teacher experiences with these programs limited their effectiveness; however, the teachers were much more optimistic for the next year's classes.

2. It was recommended that more diagnostic reading tests be given prior to grouping.

3. Administrators feel that the success or failure of the program depends largely on the ability of the teacher and the availability and use of instructional supplies.

4. Many small problems that arose may have been prevented through more intensive planning and preparation on the part of administrators and teachers.

5. More scientific methods of research could have been utilized, such as the control group with matched pairs, with follow-up studies to ascertain the results.

6. More refined methods of selecting the students for the various classes could have been utilized.

Concluding Remarks

The basic goal in the three programs described was to set up a program in which the slow learner would be given an opportunity to experience academic success in the classroom.

In general, this goal was reached, but due to such factors as inadequate selection devices, lack of teacher preparation and training, materials and supplies and a sound guiding philosophy, the success was not as great as anticipated.

There was no attempt to segregate the true slow learner from the pseudo-slow learner, that is, one who is achieving at the academic level of a slow learner but has an intellectual ability much higher. Also, the students were grouped only for reading ability. It seems reasonable to assume that there may be problems in the areas of arithmetic and language as well. It appears that the educational program for the slow learner would be quite different from that of one for the pseudo-slow learner in all subject areas, and that perhaps grouping should be flexible and based on subject-matter weakness rather than on just one subject deficiency.

The programs presented here should be considered as pilot efforts in the first stage of development; with proper refinement they may hold great promise for the education of the slow learner in the Mesa Public Schools.

Providing for Slow Learners in the Phoenix Union High Schools

We have not solved all of the problems connected with the teaching of our slow learners, but we are very much concerned about teaching them as effectively as possible. Here are some of the things we are doing to try to make learning more meaningful and valuable for them.

1. *Identification.* We begin our testing program in the eighth grades with the Cooperative Reading Tests and the Differential Aptitude Tests. The results of these tests, together with the recommendations of the eighth grade teachers and the students' academic records are then used by our counselors in helping eighth graders plan their high school programs of study. Of course, both parents and students are involved in this planning. At the time of this planning, the counselors indicate on the registration card whether a student should probably be assigned to a fast learning class, a regular class, a slow learning class, or a special education class.

2. *Grouping—Levels of Instruction.* We have four levels of instruction in our schools—Special Education, Slow, Regular, and Fast—and all classes are organized on one of these four levels. Assignment to one of these levels of instruction is based primarily on one's skills, rather than on one's general intelligence. Grouping is thus designed so that common problems may be attacked and common materials may be used at whatever rate the class works efficiently. Since some students may be slower in mathematics than in English, such students may be assigned to a Slow Learning class in mathematics, and a Regular or Fast learning class in English. Incidentally, we refer to our Fast learning classes as AA classes or "able

---

[1] By Dr. Lewis Allbee, Assistant Superintendent for Educational Services, Phoenix Union High Schools.

and ambitious" classes. Although we do not have special classes for slow learners in all subjects, we do have them in the following:

English 1-2   General Science
English 3-4   Earth and Space Science
English 5-6   Biology 1-2
English 7-8   Chemistry 1-2
World History 1-2   Spanish 1-2
American History 1-2   Spanish 3-4
American Government   General Business 1-2
Economics   Record Keeping 1-2
General Mathematics   General Clerical Practices 1-2
Business Mathematics

3. *Selection of Curriculum Materials.* As a matter of school policy, two textbooks on each of three levels (Slow, Regular, Fast) are adopted for use in those subjects having more than one level of instruction. In addition, two textbooks on each of two levels (normal readers and slow readers) may be adopted for use in each elective course in which students have a reading problem. Supplementary texts and curriculum materials are included each year in our Approved List of Basic and Supplementary High School Textbooks. If teachers wish to use a text, magazine, or some other kind of instructional material that does not appear on the approved list, this can be done subject to the approval of the Unit Head and the Chairman of the Textbook Committee.

4. *Course Outlines.* Rather complete course outlines were prepared in 1957 for slow learners in freshman and sophomore English, freshman mathematics, and senior civics and economics. These course outlines include the purposes, specific outcomes, content, learning experiences, and resources available on many topics. During the coming school year we plan to review these course outlines in order to bring them up-to-date. We also plan to develop new course outlines for those subject areas in which we do not now have them.

5. *Reading Classes.* To help many students who read at two or more years below grade level, we provide classes in remedial reading. During 1961–62 we used 10 full-time reading specialists specifically assigned to this program in our seven high schools. In addition to a remedial reading program, we initiated two

new projects in developmental reading during 1961–62. One of these projects was at South Mountain High School and involved the employment of a reading specialist to work directly with all of our ninth grade English classes. The English teachers remain with their classes while the reading specialist is working with them. The reason for this is to provide some in-service education for these teachers as well as some reading instruction for students. We expect all freshman English teachers to teach reading, and this may be a way to help them teach reading more effectively. The second project in developmental reading is at Camelback High School. Here the students in all freshman English classes have a reading specialist as a regular classroom teacher for six weeks during the year. There is no other regular teacher in the same classroom during these six weeks. The Camelback project also involves the assignment of each freshman English class to a speech specialist for six weeks during the year. Please note that both of these projects (at South Mountain and at Camelback) make reading instruction available for all freshmen: Slow, Regular, and Fast.

6. *Practical Shop.* At Phoenix Union High School we have two two-hour practical shops available for "special education" and slow-learning students. The two-fold purposes of these shops are: to provide some practical "vocational" training for special education students who may not yet be ready for on-the-job training; and to provide an opportunity for "slow-learning" students who are not qualified for regular vocational training but who very likely will drop out of school unless they have some kind of practical training to help them earn a living later on. The vocational training areas covered in these practical shops are selected from the following: repair and maintenance of household equipment, automobile painting, automobile washing, automobile sanding, use of maintenance and spray equipment, appliance painting, furniture refinishing, roller painting, landscaping, lawn care, beginning woodwork, beginning sheet metalwork, basic electricity, and beginning acetylene welding.

7. *Work Experience.* We believe that some practical work experience is good for everyone in school and especially so for students who are not academically inclined. Therefore, we have

provided the following opportunities for work experience during the school day:

a. Business work experience—for seniors in business education.

b. School work experience—for any student for a maximum of two years as audio-visual assistant, laboratory assistant, library assistant, stage-craft work, bookstore work, or clerical work for the guidance board, administrative offices, guidance offices, department heads and health centers.

c. Vocational agriculture—for students who wish to work in some agricultural pursuit.

d. Distributive education—for students who wish to go into retail selling and merchandizing.

e. Diversified occupations—will be initiated for special education students during 1961–62. We hope to have a program in diversified occupations for other students by 1962–63.

f. Trades and Industries Programs—for students wanting to learn a skilled trade. Opportunities are now provided in the following programs:

> Air Conditioning Technology 1-2, 3-4
> Aircraft Airframe 1-2, 3-4
> Aircraft Powerplants 1-2, 3-4
> Architectural Drafting 1-2, 3-4
> Auto Body & Fender 1-2, 3-4
> Auto Chassis 1-2, 3-4
> Auto Engine Repair 1-2, 3-4, 5-6
> Auto Mechanics (Basic) 1-2
> Auto Painting 1-2, 3-4
> Auto Tune-up 1-2, 3-4
> Auto Upholstery & Trimming 1-2, 3-4
> Cab. Making & Furniture Construction 1-2, 3-4
> Carpentry 1-2, 3-4
> Clothing & Design & Power Sewing 1-2, 3-4
> Commercial Art 1-2, 3-4, 5-6
> Cooking and Baking 1-2, 3-4
> **Cosmetology (8 hrs. per day—approx 11 mos.)
> ***Dental Assisting (6 hrs. per day—2 semesters)
> Diesel & Truck Mechanics 1-2, 3-4
> ***Drafting Technology 1-2, 3-4
> ***Electronics Technology 1-2, 3-4
> Furniture Upholstery 1-2, 3-4
> Industrial Electricity 1-2, 3-4, 5-6
> Machine Shop 1-2, 3-4, 5-6

**Students enrolling in Cosmetology and Practical Nursing must be 17 years of age and must have completed a minimum of two years of high school.
***The programs for Dental Assisting, Drafting Technology, Tool & Die Technology and Electronics Technology are open only to high school seniors and graduates.

Mechanical Drafting 1-2, 3-4
**Practical Nursing (6 hrs. per day—12 mos.)
Refrigeration & Air Conditioning 1-2, 3-4, 5-6
Radio Service 1-2, 3-4
Sheet Metal 1-2, 3-4, 5-6
Television Service 1-2, 3-4
***Tool & Die Technology 1-2
Vocational Agriculture 1-2, 3-4, 5-6
Welding—Arc & Acetylene 1-2, 3-4, 5-6

8. *Supervisory Assistance.* Good supervisory assistance is helpful in promoting better programs for slow learners as well as for all other learners. We have been fortunate during the past few years in being able to add to our staff a number of outstanding teachers who are assigned a minimum of half-time to working with other teachers. By next year we expect to provide such assistance in the following areas: English, social studies, mathematics, science, business, home economics, and industrial arts.

9. *In-Service Education.* The more in-service education a school system provides, the better the chances are that the slow learners will receive the attention they deserve. During the past year we have had four half-days of released time for all teachers devoted to in-service education. Next year we expect to have four more half-days of released time for all teachers. In addition, we have a sizeable budget for professional travel, bringing in of educational consultants, and the development of up-to-date curriculum materials for all to use.

10. *Summer Workshops.* One of our most valuable ways of providing for slow learners is through summer workshops for teachers. For example, in past summers we held the following workshops:

World History—11 teachers for 2 weeks.
Special Education—13 teachers for 2 weeks.
TV for Senior Social Studies—9 teachers for 2 weeks.
English AA—27 teachers for 2 weeks.

During the summer of 1961 we held the following workshops for teachers:

Physical Sciences —14 teachers for 2 weeks.
Special Education —14 teachers for 2 weeks.
Foreign Languages — 8 teachers for 3 weeks.
Foods Workshop   — 8 teachers for 2 weeks.

| English | —12 teachers for 1 week. |
| Social Studies | — 7 teachers for 2 weeks. |

During the summer of 1962 our workshop was concerned with the development of a first-class program for Slow General Mathematics. All of us involved in the instructional programs in our schools realize that meeting the needs of slow learners is one of our most urgent problems. Therefore, in the years ahead much of our time, thought, and effort will be focused on learning how we may help these youngsters to benefit to the maximum from their high school programs of study and work experience.

Index

Index

School practices (*Cont.*)
  curriculum, 64–69
  grading policies, 62–63
  promotion policies, 62–63
  special classes, 63–64
  teachers, 73–75
  teaching techniques, 69–72
Science (*see* Curriculum)
Secondary school, 24, 52, 57–61
Sexton, Patricia Cayo, 8, 54
Slums and Suburbs, Conant, 8, 10, 45, 46
Smith, Marion Funk, 6
Social studies (*see* Curriculum)
Socio-economic factors (*see* Deprivation)
Special classes, 63–64
Stendler, Celia Burns, 8
Stout, Irving W., 43
Strang, Ruth, 43
Subject-matter fields (*see* Curriculum)
Symonds, Percival M., 26

T

Taylor, Katherine Whiteside, 41
Teachers of slow learners, 31, 53, 73–75

Teachers of slow learners (*Cont.*)
  in-service preparation, 51, 107–108
  qualifications, 73–74
Teaching Reading to Slow Learning Children, Kirk, 19, 58, 67
Teaching the Slow Learner, Featherstone, 2, 55, 73, 79
Teaching techniques, 69–72
Team teaching, 70–71
Techniques of teaching (*see* Teaching techniques)
Tests, 10, 11, 13–14, 20–21
Trump, J. Lloyd, 71
Tucker, Ruel E., 59

U

Ungraded primary, 55

V

Vocational education, 59, 105–106

W

White, Verna, 22
White House Conference on Children and Youth, 10, 48, 49, 72